D1113390

< HOW TO DO THINGS WITH VIDEOGAMES >

HOW
TO DO
THINGS
WITH
VIDEOGAMES

Ian Bogost

Electronic Mediations 38

University of Minnesota Press

Minneapolis

London

Published by the University of Minnesota Press
111 Third Avenue South, Suite 290
Minneapolis, MN 55401-2520
http://www.upress.umn.edu

Library of Congress Cataloging-in-Publication Data

Bogost, Ian.
   How to do things with videogames / Ian Bogost.
      p.   cm. — (Electronic mediations ; v. 38)
   Includes bibliographical references and index.
   ISBN 978-0-8166-7646-0 (hc : alk. paper)
   ISBN 978-0-8166-7647-7 (pb : alk. paper)
   1. Video games—Social aspects. I. Title.
   GV1469.34.S52B63   2011
   793.93'2—dc23

                                          2011023625

Printed in the United States of America on acid-free paper

The University of Minnesota is an equal-opportunity educator and employer.

18 17 16 15 14 13 12 11   10 9 8 7 6 5 4 3 2

Contents

Media Microecology

These days, you can't open a website or enter a bookstore without finding yet another impassioned take on emerging technologies' promise to change our lives for the better—or for the worse. For every paean to Wikipedia or blogging or mobile computing, there's an equally vehement condemnation.

On one side of one such contest, the journalist Nicholas Carr argues that the Internet has contributed to a decline in the careful, reasoned, imaginative mind of the period between the Renaissance and the Industrial Revolution.[1] Though we may feel that we're "getting smarter" by grazing across multiple bits of knowledge, Carr suggests that this feeling is a fleeting one, the burst of energy from a sugary snack instead of lasting nourishment from a wholesome meal.

Carr's book about the problem, titled *The Shallows,* hit store shelves at the same time as Clay Shirky's *Cognitive Surplus,* which argues just the opposite: the social power of those tiny snippets Carr reviles. In a characteristic example, Shirky describes South Korean protests against the reintroduction of U.S.-raised beef after the mad cow disease scare of the early 2000s. Surprisingly, the uprising was fueled not by radical agitators or by media pundits but by fans of the Korean boy band Dong Ban Shin Ki, whose website forums became, in Shirky's words, "a locus of coordination."[2]

Carr's and Shirky's accounts provide two opposing takes on the value of reading and writing excerpts online. Who's right? It's a question that drives blog commenters, talk show banter, and book sales, to be sure. But things aren't quite so simple, and reflection on both positions should make either one feel incomplete on its own.

< 1 >

As Matthew Battles has argued, Carr seems to assume that reading is monolithic. "Dipping and skimming," Battles reminds us, "have been modes available to readers for ages. Carr makes one kind of reading—literary reading, specifically—into the only kind that matters. But these and other modes of reading have long coexisted, feeding one another, needing one another."[3] Skimming isn't just something we do with literary texts, either: we also skim menus, signs, magazines, and countless other textual objects. It shouldn't be any surprise that reading is a varied activity. And besides, the isolated, single-sense, top-down, purportedly truth-bearing process of reading after Johannes Gutenberg is also precisely the aspect of print culture Marshall McLuhan lamented three decades *before* the Web.[4]

On the flipside, when he celebrates the Korean boy band forum uprising, Shirky makes his own assumptions. In particular, he takes for granted that the will of the people matters above all else. Whether the end of a five-year ban on U.S. beef in Korea really ever posed a health threat to the population isn't of much concern to Shirky; rather, the emergence of unexpected, collaborative discourse is his primary interest. Shirky assumes that the potential collective impact of online communications justifies the more mundane and, as Carr would have it, pointless uses of media—like swooning over boy bands.

Carr's worry about the Web's tendency to encourage skin-deep thinking about unimportant subjects does ring true. But Shirky's account of the surprisingly political amalgam of all those seemingly useless, skin-deep comments also demands acknowledgment. As with most best-seller list disagreements about culture, both Carr's and Shirky's takes make broad, far-reaching claims of impact: either the Internet is ruining society or it is rescuing it. Here's a different, less flashy answer: technology neither saves nor condemns us. It influences us, of course, changing how we perceive, conceive of, and interact with our world. McLuhan calls a medium an *extension of ourselves* for just this reason: it structures and informs our understanding and behavior.[5] But the

Internet extends us in both remarkable and unremarkable ways. From keeping a journal to paying a bill to reminiscing about an old television advertisement, the Web offers just as many mundane uses as it does remarkable ones. Probably more.

That's not a popular sentiment in our time of technological spectacularism. It wouldn't play well in a TED talk or on a *Wired* cover. But I'm going to insist on it as a media philosophy: we can understand the relevance of a medium by looking at the variety of things it does.

It's a fact true of all media, not just computers. Think of all the things you can do with a photograph. You can document the atrocities and celebrations of war, as did photojournalists like Eddie Adams and Alfred Eisenstaedt. You can record fleeting moments in time, as did photographers like Henri Cartier-Bresson and Robert Frank. You can capture the ordinary moments of family life, as all of us do at birthday parties or holidays for an album or shoebox archive. You can take a snapshot reminder of a home improvement project to help you buy the right part at the hardware store. An automated camera at a street intersection can capture a license plate for ticketing, and a pornographer can capture a naked body for titillation. Photography has common properties— it bends light through an aperture to expose an emulsion or digital sensor. But the uses of photography vary widely. It is this breadth and depth of uses that makes photography a mature medium.

We can think of a medium's explored uses as a spectrum, a possibility space that extends from purely artistic uses at one end (the decisive moment photograph) to purely instrumental uses at the other (the hardware store snapshot). In a given medium, many of these uses are known and well explored, while others are new and emerging. One way to grasp a medium's cultural influence is to examine how much of that field of uses has been explored. This approach represents a shift in how we encounter media artifacts as creators, users, and critics.

Carr's and Shirky's books show us just how far the media ecological approach has come since McLuhan popularized it in the 1960s. He suggested that we study the *properties* of a medium rather than the individual *messages* produced by media, thus the famous aphorism "the medium is the message."[6] His point was that the things a medium does to a culture are more important than the content it conveys. For example, McLuhan argued that the printing press ushered in an era of visual culture and that the mass-produced book homogenized experience and knowledge. Photographs allow light to be recorded on photosensitive film. Telegraphs allow words to be transmitted over long distances. Paintings allow pigmented substances to cover surfaces. Where once our understanding of media was limited to their representational aspects (the meaning of a photograph, film, or novel), McLuhan's influence helped steer scholarly, journalistic, and public attention toward the effects a medium exerts on society (the way the Web changes how we think, socialize, work, and play). Both *The Shallows* and *Cognitive Surplus* take a media ecological approach, offering strong positions on the positive or negative effects of the Internet on human culture.

Understanding the properties of a medium *does* help us better comprehend their nature and their implications. Videogames, the subject of this book, also have properties that precede their content: games are models of experiences rather than textual descriptions or visual depictions of them. When we play games, we operate those models, our actions constrained by their rules: the urban dynamics of *SimCity*; the feudal stealth strategy of *Ninja Gaiden*; the racing tactics of *Gran Turismo*. On top of that, we take on a role in a videogame, putting ourselves in the shoes of someone else: the urban planner, the ninja, the auto racer. Videogames are a medium that lets us play a role within the constraints of a model world. And unlike playground games or board games, videogames are computational, so the model worlds and sets of rules they produce can be far more complex. These properties—computational models and roles—help us understand how videogames work and how they are different from other media.

But the media ecological approach alone gets us only so far. For example, many misconceptions surround videogames. All-too-familiar questions arise about whether games promote violent action or whether they make us fat through inactivity. Such accusations stem partly from overly general assumptions about a medium's content and reception (which, in the case of videogames, is assumed to be violent scenarios that induce aggression). But they also emerge from overly general assumptions about a medium's properties and the contexts in which those properties get deployed.

The content and context of a media artifact is not as inessential as McLuhan would have it. The medium is the message, but the message is the message, too. Instead of ignoring it, we ought to explore the relationships between the general properties of a medium and the particular situations in which it is used.

A recent trend in videogames helps drive the point home. Hoping to overturn the idea that games are only for entertainment, *serious games* claim to offer an alternative: games that can be used "outside entertainment" in education, health care, or corporate training, for example.[7] For serious games proponents, videogames' ability to create worlds in which players take on roles constrained by rules offers excellent opportunities for new kinds of learning. While indeed worthwhile, this media ecological perspective risks collapsing into a mirror image of accusations that videogames can only encourage violence and sloth. Serious games play the role of Clay Shirky to videogame detractors' Nicholas Carr. Once more, technology either saves or seduces us.

Games—like photography, like writing, like any medium—shouldn't be shoehorned into one of two kinds of uses, serious or superficial, highbrow or lowbrow, useful or useless. Neither entertainment nor seriousness nor the two together should be a satisfactory account for what videogames are capable of. After all, we don't distinguish between only two kinds of books, or music, or photography, or film. Rather, we know intuitively that writing, sound, images, and moving pictures can all be put to many different uses. A voice can whisper an amorous sentiment or mount a political stump speech. A book can carry us off to a fantasy world or help us decide where to eat dinner. A television program can shock us with an account of genocide or help us practice aerobics.

Such an attitude requires us to expand our understanding of media ecology. In McLuhan's terms, the media ecosystem entails "arranging various media to help each other so they won't cancel each other out, to buttress one medium with another."[8] In other words, media ecology is a general, media-agnostic approach to understanding how a host of different technologies works individually and together to create an environment for communication and perception. Traditionally, media ecologists have explored their subject at a level equivalent to the global ecosystem, concerned with how particular technologies change the overall style and quality of life. Here's Neil Postman on the subject:

> If you remove the caterpillar from a given habitat, you are left not with the same environment minus caterpillars: you have a new environment, and you have reconstituted the conditions of survival. . . . In the year 1500, fifty years after the printing press was invented, we did not have old Europe plus the printing press. We had a different Europe. After television, the United States was not America plus television; television gave a new coloration to every political campaign, to every home, to every school, to every church, to every industry.[9]

Keeping the biological metaphor, the *individual* range of functions afforded by a particular medium's properties could be compared to a *microhabitat*, a small, specialized environment within a larger ecosystem. Postman's caterpillar is not merely an aspect of the woods but also an agent in its own right, one that relates to leaves, logs, and pollen. Indeed, the dedicated media ecologist must be concerned not only with the *overall* ecosystem but also with the distinctive functions of its components. *Media microecology*, we might call it. Such an approach sometimes requires a more specialized and perhaps a less glamorous method: like the ecologist reveals the unseen purposes of a decomposing log, so the media ecologist must do with particular media forms.

Following the lead of media ecologists like McLuhan and Postman, media microecology seeks to reveal the impact of a medium's properties on society. But it does so through a more specialized, focused attention to a single medium, digging deep into one dark, unexplored corner of a media ecosystem, like an ecologist digs deep into the natural one. Just as an entomologist might create a collection that thoroughly characterizes the types, roles, and effects of insects on an environment, so a media microecologist might do the same for a medium. In doing so, the value of that medium (the sort of question authors like Carr and Shirky pose) is less important than the documentation of its variety and application. For it is only after conducting such an investigation that we should feel qualified to consider distinct varieties of a medium as promising or threatening to a particular way of life. And indeed, after doing so, we might well feel less certain of such definitive moral positions anyway.

In this book, I attempt such an effort for videogames. Its goal is to reveal a small portion of the many uses of videogames, and how together they make the medium broader, richer, and more relevant. I take for granted that understanding games as a medium of leisure or productivity alone is insufficient. Instead, I suggest we imagine the videogame as a medium with valid uses across the spectrum, from art to tools and everything in between. I won't assume that the best or most legitimate specimens are still to come, or that laying a groundwork for designers, markets, players, or critics will help them realize the videogame's potential in some revelatory master work. Instead I'll take for granted that videogames are already becoming a pervasive medium, one as interwoven with culture as writing and images. Videogames are not a subcultural form meant for adolescents but just another medium woven into everyday life.

Yet most of us haven't begun to think about games in this way, as a medium with many uses that together pervade contemporary life, and as a result, interesting adoptions of the form have been labeled illegitimate or simply ignored. In the short essays that follow, I cover myriad examples of applications for, sensations of, and experiences with videogames. In each, I hope to show how videogames have seeped out of our computers and become enmeshed in our lives. I offer these essays not as a complete catalog of videogames' present or future potential but as a starting point for us to think about how to do things with videogames.

1 Art

Are videogames art? It's a question that's sparked considerable debate, most notably thanks to the film critic Roger Ebert's declaration that "the nature of the medium prevents it from moving beyond craftsmanship to the stature of art."[1] For the philosopher and game designer Jim Preston, it's an absurd and useless question:

> To think that there is a single, generally agreed upon concept of art is to get it precisely backwards. Americans' attitude towards art is profoundly divided, disjointed and confused; and my message to gamers is to simply ignore the "is-it-art?" debate altogether.[2]

Preston sheds light on a fatal problem with the "games as art" conversation. Forget games, *art* doesn't have any sort of stable meaning in contemporary culture anyway.

There are many reasons for such a development, perhaps the most important being that the twentieth-century avant-garde changed art for good. In the turbulent times of the first two decades of the last century, localized movements in Europe gained attention by rejecting traditionalism. Futurism's founder Filippo Marinetti spurned all things old and embraced youth, machine, violence. Then when violence became reality in World War I, a handful of artists in Zurich concluded that if progress since the Enlightenment had led to the destruction of the Great War, then such progress had to be rejected. They called their work Dada. The futurists called for a total reinvention of cultural and political life.

< 9 >

Dada scorned artistic and social conventions in favor of absurd-ism and recontextualization. Tristan Tzara performed live poetry by choosing words randomly out of a hat. Marcel Duchamp made a urinal into art by putting it in a gallery rather than a bathroom.

Movements like these, which collectively became known as the *avant-garde*, disrupted traditional notions of art's role and context. As the last century wore on, it became much harder to distinguish art by its form or function alone; context became the predominant factor, its arbitrariness exposed forever by Duchamp's urinal.

But even before the avant-garde, the history of art is strewn with the babes and corpses of movements that hoped to reimagine or reinvent their predecessors, even if they did so less rapidly. The Gothic style of the twelfth through fourteenth centuries preferred elongation, ornament, and angles in sculpture, architecture, and painting. The Renaissance perfected perspective. Realism of the late nineteenth and early twentieth centuries focused on portray-als of everyday life, itself spawning numerous movements of their own right such as postimpressionism and the Pre-Raphaelites. From the long perspective of history, the very idea that "art" means something monolithic and certain is absurd, as Preston suspects.

What lessons can videogames learn, even from a rudimentary understanding of art history? For starters, there are no unified field theories of art. The pursuit of a pure, single account of art in any medium is a lost cause. Instead, the history of art has been one of disruption and reinvention, one of conflicting trends and ideas within each historical period, and since the nineteenth cen-tury even more so.

After all, the twentieth century saw the following things enjoy celebration as fine art: a urinal placed on a stand; a painting of a colored square; poetry made of words drawn randomly from a hat; an audience that cuts the clothes off an artist; industrial paint thrown onto canvas; reproductions of commercial adver-tisements; a telegram sent to a recipient it claims to portray; a bar-ricade of oil barrels on a Paris street; a continuous live television image of a Buddha statue. Lest one conclude that such examples are outlandish edge cases, consider the artists who produced them: Duchamp, Piet Mondrian, Tzara, Yoko Ono, Jackson Pollock, Andy Warhol, Robert Rauschenberg, Christo and Jeanne-Claude, Nam Jun Paik, respectively. All are celebrated as major figures, whose status as artists would never be questioned. They demonstrate that "art" is hardly a fixed and uncontroversial topic. Art has done many things in human history, but in the last century especially, it has primarily tried to bother and provoke us. To force us to see things differently. Art changes. Its very purpose, we might say, is to change, and to change us along with it.

How then can we understand the role of games in art? Satisfying Ebert's challenge that games simply need to get up off their proverbial couches and rise up to the authorial status of literature or film is not the way forward.[3] Neither is the impassioned folly of appeals to videogames' legal status as speech, a common counterargument among videogame apologists. Nor still is the repurposing of familiar game imagery as folk art homage, in crafts for sale on Etsy.com or as cakes featured on videogame blogs. Nor indeed is granting gallery status to game stills and concept art by hanging them in exhibitions at trade conventions, as has been done at the main videogame retailers trade show, Electronic Entertainment Expo, for many years.

Despite its lack of specificity, the idea of "games as art," or *art-games,* to use the designer Jason Rohrer's term, does offer some insight on its own. It suggests that games can be construed *natively* as art, within the communities of practice and even the industry of games, rather than by pledging fealty to the fine art kingdom. Its practitioners are game developers first, working artists second, if at all. By contrast, the term *game art* describes a work prepared for exhibition in galleries or museums, still the "traditional" venues for art despite Duchamp. Cory Arcangel's *Super Mario Clouds,* a hack of the Nintendo Entertainment System cart that removes everything but the moving clouds, offers a good example of game art.[4] These are games that get exhibited, not games that get played.

Beyond such a distinction, however, and despite its rhetorical power, *artgame* is an insufficient term to be useful for players, creators, or critics. It is a stand-in for a yet unnamed set of movements or styles, akin to realism or futurism. We must look deeper, to the particularities of specific aesthetic trends in game development itself, in hopes of identifying their positions in relation to games and art alike. In other words, what we lack are discussions of the developing conventions, styles, movements through which games are participating in a broader concept of art, both locally and historically. There are many such styles we might consider, so let's choose one to focus on.

Consider Rohrer, Jonathan Blow, and Rod Humble, three figures whose names often arise in discussions of games and art, and whose work each contains a game about the nature of human relationships. Their work embraces simplicity of representation bent neither toward the pixellated pang of nostalgia nor the formal austerity of abstract emergence. I suggest the term *proceduralism* to characterize the style represented partly by these three and a few others. It is not a name for all games, nor all artgames, nor perhaps even all games by the creators just mentioned. Instead, it is a name for a style they have embraced deliberately and successfully.

Blow's game *Braid* takes the seemingly familiar genre of the platformer and turns it into an allegorical exploration of the themes of time and regret. At the game's start, it sets up a seemingly familiar situation in which the player character Tim is meant to rescue a princess from a monster. But the relationship between the two is quickly revealed to be more complex than this standard videogame trope allows. The game offers its player the ability to rewind time, allowing recovery from mistakes (there is no death in *Braid*), while creating new implications for platform puzzles in different sets of levels. In one world, certain objects are unaffected by time manipulation. In another, character movement to the right moves time forward, and movement to the left moves it in reverse.

Rohrer's *Passage* is an abstract *memento mori*. The player controls a man who moves through an abstract, pixellated world. The player can choose to couple with a female character near the game's start, in which case the two move together as one for the rest of the game, or to return later after exploring the mazelike environment. Throughout, treasure chests are scattered, some of which open to reveal stars, others dust. Capturing stars from chests constructs memories that can be seen later. Over time, the characters age and change appearance, their hair color, clothing, gait, and speed of movement reflecting their progression through life, and finally they die, first the woman and then the man after her. The entire process takes place over five minutes.

And Humble's game *The Marriage* offers an even more abstract take on romantic coupling, offering no concrete representation save the work's title. In the game, two large squares, one blue and one pink, representing a man and a woman, move about a 2-D field. Circles of various colors enter and leave the space. The interactions between squares, circles, and the player's mouse create different consequences for the blue and pink squares. For example, mousing over either square reduces the size of the blue one and moves the two closer together. The pink square becomes more transparent over time, but when it touches any colored circle save black, it increases in size. When either square reduces to nothing or becomes completely transparent, the game ends. The game, in Humble's words, "is my expression of how a marriage feels."[5]

While quite different in nature, *Braid, Passage,* and *The Marriage* share several common properties, some related to desired effect, some related to method of creation, and some related to form. I suggest five: procedural rhetoric, introspection, abstraction, subjective representation, and strong authorship.

As the name implies, proceduralist games are process intensive—they rely primarily on computational rules to produce their artistic meaning. In these games, expression arises primarily from the player's interaction with the game's mechanics and dynamics, and less so (in some cases almost not at all) in their visual, aural, and textual aspects. These games lay bare the form, allowing meaning to emanate from a model.

Elsewhere, I have given the term *procedural rhetoric* to an argument made through a computer model.[6] A procedural rhetoric makes a claim about how something works by modeling its processes in the process-native environment of the computer rather than using description (writing) or depiction (images). When it relates to games intended to change opinions, this term coheres well enough. But it has introduced some confusion in other contexts, probably owing to the unpopularity of the term *rhetoric* in contemporary culture—for many, it's just a synonym for *lies*. But for the rhetorician, the term characterizes the process of expression much more broadly.

In artgames like the three in question, a procedural rhetoric does not argue a position but rather characterizes an idea. These games say something about how an experience of the world works, how it feels to experience or to be subjected to some sort of situation: marriage, mortality, regret, confusion, and so forth.

Proceduralist games are oriented toward introspection over both immediate gratification, as is usually the case in entertainment games, and external action, whether immediate or deferred, as is usually the case in serious games. The goal of the proceduralist designer is to cause the player to reflect on one or more themes during or after play, without a concern for resolution or effect. The use of identifiably human yet still abstract roles in these games underscores the invitation to project one's own experiences and ideas on them.

Passage, for example, is a game about life's choices, lessons, and inevitable end. Because it's abstract in its representation of partnership and the passage from youth to old age to death, it inspires, quite naturally, consideration of this process. *The Marriage* is about the push and pull of maintaining a relationship, but the significance of that theme sits in the ambiguity between its title and the behaviors it implements. These games pose questions about life and simulate specific experiences in response, but those experiences rarely point players toward definitive answers.

Their focus on meaning in mechanics notwithstanding, proceduralist games do not reject graphics, sound, text, or even story entirely. But when they do include such things, these games tend to reject verisimilitude in favor of abstraction.

Part of the reason for this is practical, as these games are often created by one or two people. But a more important reason is aesthetic: reducing the player's obsession with decoration under-scores the experience of processes while still allowing image, sound, and text to meaningfully clarify the fiction of the game's theme. Although one common method for abstraction is 2-D ren-dering (as is the case in *Braid*, *Passage*, and *The Marriage*), not all proceduralist games adopt this perspective. Mike Treanor's *Reflect* offers an example of a 3-D proceduralist work, a game about the movement of creatures small and large. Treanor's choice of a seemingly retrograde, low polygon-count rendering style serves an aesthetic rather than nostalgic purpose: it de-emphasizes vi-sual fidelity in favor of the experience of movement. As far as story is concerned, procedural works tend to employ metaphor or vi-gnette instead of narrative. Daniel Benmergui's *Storyteller* offers an instructive example: the game tells a tale through the causal relationships between different characters, at different times, in accordance with their position on a triptychlike stage.

No matter the level of abstraction, proceduralist works don't equate higher abstraction with lower production value. Where image, sound, and text is present, it's carefully selected and in-corporated into the system that forms the rest of the game—the time-reversible background particles in Blow's *Braid*; the ex-pressive six-pixel eyes in Benmergui's *I Wish I Were the Moon*; the logarithmically scaled distortion of past and future vision in Rohrer's *Passage*. Such assets are always tightly coupled to the gameplay itself.

Games like *Go* and *Tetris* are abstract; if they have any about-ness, it is limited to the experience of the system itself. One can make representational claims about these games (Janet Murray has called *Tetris* "the perfect enactment of the overtasked lives of Americans"), but only in an overtly metaphoric way.[7] By contrast, games like *SimCity* and *Madden* are concrete; they deal with specific subjects and activities, in this case urban planning and American football.

Proceduralist games sit between these two poles. Their systems characterize a subject not by accident of genre or convention but through deliberate selection—often inspired by a solitary creator's personal experience. At the same time, proceduralist works are not as clear about their representations as are other games. There's an ambiguity of both form and signification in these works. Another example of the style, Bernhard Schulenburg's *Where Is My Heart,* demonstrates both of these aspects. The game deals with "the complication of family life" by distributing success among three abstract characters and jumbling an intricate platformer world about the screen.

From the perspective of form, proceduralist artgames tend to combine concrete, identifiable situations with abstract tokens, objects, goals, or actions, like the abstract tokens in Rohrer's treasure chests. From the perspective of signification, proceduralist works deploy a more poetic and less direct way to express the ideas or scenarios their processes represent. *Braid* poses questions about doubt, forgiveness, time, and regret, offering the player an opportunity to pursue the question, "what if I could go back," in different ways. But the answers to these questions are not presented as definitive solutions discovered automatically through mastery of the game's system. In this sense, proceduralism shares some of the values of expressionism in art, especially as both relate to the subjective interpretation of emotion.

When we ponder the subjective themes of human experience, it's hard to do so in relation to the nameless anonymity of corporate creation. Thus the strong presence of a human author is prevalent in these games, whether an individual or individually identified members of a small group.

The concept of authorship incorporates another feature of art more broadly: the pursuit of a particular truth irrespective of the demands of reception or sales. The sense that the artifact has something to relate and will not relent until that thing is expressed, rather than an experience to be optimized, is at work here. Still, we must not mistake authorship for intention. The intentional fallacy, which rejects the idea that a work's meaning or value is related to the creator's intention, is still at work in games. Player agency in games of all kinds leads to unique interpretations of play experiences; in proceduralist works, such meaning generation is spurred by the knowledge that a specific human being set the work's processes into motion.

Artistic styles, movements, and traditions sometimes arrive via the declaration of a group of artists, as was the case with the manifestos of the early twentieth century. Indeed, the Belgian artist duo known as Tale of Tales penned a "Realtime Art Manifesto" in 2006 to describe and rally interest around their style, which differs considerably from that of proceduralism: they reject rules and goals in favor of high-gloss, low-interaction 3-D experiences and situations.[8] In other cases, critics and historians describe the emergence and evolution of a style during or after the fact. Whether the creators mentioned above would embrace the *proceduralist* is an open question, but such a matter need not undermine the usefulness of describing a style in the process of maturation.

As a style, proceduralism takes a stand contrary to conventional wisdom in game design. At a time when videogames focus on realistically simulating experiences, proceduralism offers metaphoric treatments of ideas. At a time when videogames focus on player gratification, proceduralism invites player introspection. At a time when videogames focus on facilitating user creativity, proceduralism lays bare the subjective truth of an individual creator. It is not the only artistic movement in games, but as one with a coherent set of goals and aesthetics, it serves much the same purpose as did futurism or Dada: to issue a specific challenge to a medium from within it. And that if nothing else is most certainly a feature of art.

2

Empathy

One of the unique properties of videogames is their ability to put us in someone else's shoes. But most of the time, those shoes are bigger than our own. When we play videogames, we resemble children clopping around in their parent's loafers or pumps, imagining what it would be like to see over the kitchen counter. In many cases, these roles fulfill power fantasies. Videogames let us wield deadly weapons. They let us wage intergalactic war. They let us take a shot on goal in the World Cup final. They let us build cities, and then they let us destroy them. But powerful roles are not the only ones games afford.

Darfur Is Dying, created by Susana Ruiz as part of her MFA thesis at the University of Southern California, is a game that breaks this tradition. In one part of the game, the player takes the role of a Darfuri child who ventures out of the village to a well to retrieve water for his family. To accomplish this task, the player must run across a sparse desert in search of a well, and then back again, while avoiding jeeps of Janjaweed militia that easily overtake the slower, more vulnerable child. The player can hide temporarily behind shrubs and desert trash, but staying still for too long leads to inevitable capture.

On first blush, it would be tempting to call *Darfur Is Dying* a stealth action game. This common subgenre of the action/adventure game rewards covert action over overt action. In *Thief,* the player's character must hide in the shadows while pilfering mansions. In *Splinter Cell* and *Metal Gear Solid,* the player must obscure evidence of his or her actions, such as by asphyxiating guards and hiding their bodies. And in *Deus Ex,* the player can

< 18 >

choose whether or not to be stealthy, such as by hacking a computer to pass a locked door or by killing a guard to gain passage. *Darfur Is Dying* offers a similar challenge: the player must avoid contact with militia, either by evading them or hiding behind barriers. But it lacks a feature crucial to the stealth action genre. In stealth games, covertness is a skill imbued with power. The thief's furtiveness and the secret agent's craftiness are honed abilities that separate them from the brutes they battle against.

Conversely, stealth is a weakness in *Darfur Is Dying*. The player's character hides because he or she *must* do so to survive, not because doing so gives him or her an advantage over an orthogonally powerful enemy. The player does not sneak, he or she cowers.

Among contemporary commercial videogames, the closest comparison to the experience of weakness in *Darfur Is Dying* might be found in *The Legend of Zelda: Wind Waker*. In the opening stages of that game, the protagonist travels to the Forbidden Fortress to confront his sister's kidnapper. But since he is too weak to combat the enemies he faces there, the player must instead hide in dark corners and inside barrels to pass unnoticed. Later in the game, the player returns to the Forbidden Fortress, much more powerful and experienced than before. And it is here that *Wind Waker* differs from *Darfur Is Dying*: weakness-enforced stealth in *Wind Waker* accentuates the player's future growth in power: enemies who previously overwhelmed the player are easily defeated. In *Darfur Is Dying*, weakness is all the player ever gets. There is no magic to invoke, no heroic lineage to appeal to; strength adequate to survive is simply inaccessible.

If a game about the Sudanese genocide is meant to foster empathy for terrible real-world situations in which the players fortunate enough to play videogames might intervene, then those games would do well to invite us to step into the smaller, more uncomfortable shoes of the downtrodden rather than the larger, more well-heeled shoes of the powerful.

I've attempted to implement such a strategy in some of my own games, albeit in the service of less geopolitically charged topics than sub-Saharan African politics. For example, in *Disaffected!*, a parody of Kinko's, the player is stripped of the power to service customers successfully (a feature common to order-fulfillment games from *Tapper* to *Diner Dash*). Instead, one is forced to perform under the powerlessness of alienated labor.

Darfur Is Dying and *Disaffected!* notwithstanding, operationalized weakness is not new to games. In *Ico*, for example, the player takes responsibility for an almost helpless companion. But we can trace the dynamic back much farther, to one of the most maligned titles in videogame history: *E.T. the Extra-Terrestrial* for the Atari Video Computer System (VCS).

In 1982 Atari paid Steven Spielberg $20 million to license the right to make a game based on the popular film.[1] To take advantage of the film's hype, Atari persuaded *Yars' Revenge* programmer Howard Scott Warshaw to complete the game in only five weeks, the deadline necessary to ship for Christmas. The result was widely panned for terrible gameplay and unintuitive controls. Many of the millions of cartridges that Atari printed came back unsold, and the company eventually had hundreds of thousands of *E.T.* cartridges crushed and buried in a landfill in the New Mexico desert.[2] Along with the abysmal and equally overproduced VCS adaptation of *Pac-Man*, *E.T.* is often blamed for the videogame industry crash of 1983.

No matter their frequency, complaints about *E.T.* assume that games must fulfill roles of power, that they must put us in shoes bigger than our own, and that we must be satisfied with those roles. But Spielberg's film was not about the terrific power of aliens invading—the title character, it should be noted, was a space botanist, not a space invader. It is a movie about the isolation of one alien who remained. In the face of a world that perceives E.T. as an implicit threat, a few children attempt to understand him on his own terms. It was a film about alienation, not about aliens.

Warshaw's videogame respected this core principle, whether or not it meant to. In the game, the player cannot easily predict the topology of the virtual landscape, and he or she often falls into wells. Once at the bottom of a well, the player can use E.T.'s ability to levitate to rise up and continue. While this feature of the game is universally panned for causing intense frustration, it also brilliantly juxtaposes E.T.'s purported powers with his actual weaknesses. Levitation, an ability that another game might deploy for advantage in combat, becomes a small victory that merely allows E.T. (and the player) to realize the possibility to be hunted. Once back above ground, the FBI agents and scientists give E.T. chase. And as in the film, the alien has no power to combat these foes. Just like cowering as a child in *Darfur Is Dying,* playing the role of E.T. is an expression of weakness, not of power.

Darfur Is Dying is part role-play, part simulation. First the player takes the role of a displaced Darfuri child trying to retrieve water and avoid Janjaweed militia patrols. But if successful, the game becomes a management game, in which the player must use this water to grow crops and assist hut builders. Even though the camp management game bears more similarity to traditional titles—using resources and time wisely—the water-fetching part of *Darfur Is Dying* feels more effective as a game about genocide. The management game's social rationalism betrays the sense of emotion portrayed in the water-fetching game.

USC MFA students Jamie Antonisse and Devon Johnson heeded this lesson from their forerunner. Their game *Hush* also creates a personal experience of a complex historical genocide, this time, the 1994 slaughters of the Rwandan civil war.

Hush's creators recognized that *Darfur Is Dying* successfully focuses on a singular, personal experience as a solitary approach to the topic of genocide. The game is about a Rwandan Tutsi mother trying to calm and quiet a baby to avoid discovery by Hutu soldiers. Its gameplay attempts to simulate patience. It's a rhythm game, but one that demands slow response rather than the fast action of *Dance Dance Revolution* or *Guitar Hero.* Letters corresponding with song lyrics fade in and out. Pressing the correct key at the apex of brightness registers a successful hush. Pressing too early or too late fails to calm the child, and its crying increases.

Hush is a short game; it takes around five minutes to play, maybe longer for players who take a while to acclimate in the how-to at the beginning. Allowing the child's crying to increase too much alerts a passing Hutu patrol, and the screen fades to red, a not-so-subtle implication of the pair's bloody end. Successfully working through each "level," which corresponds with a word of the lullaby, ends the game, as the Hutu patrol passes.

Darfur Is Dying and *E.T.* offer holistic experiences: the player has direct control of a character, even if that character's abilities are severely limited. *Hush* works differently, using illustrations and broadcast-style motion graphics as a stage-setting tool, to create ambience. Well-crafted, stylized renderings of documentary imagery and sounds from Rwanda of the early 1990s give a sense of the time and place. The static woodcut-style image of mother and baby are the only figures who remain static throughout the game.

If *Darfur Is Dying* and *E.T.* emphasize the role-playing property of videogames, *Hush* emphasizes the world-building property. But it does so in an unusual way: not by re-creating a vivid, realistic environment but by suggesting one. *Hush* is a vignette rather than a simulation.

In literature, poetry, and film, a vignette is a brief, indefinite, evocative description or account of a person or situation. Vignettes are usually meant to give a sense of a character rather than to advance a narrative. As in a literary sketch, vignettes are impressionistic and poetic, depicting an experience or environment, roughly, softly, and subtly.

As an aesthetic, the vignette is rare in videogames. One reason might be the relative scarcity of small-form representations of human or natural experience in the medium. Minigames like those of the *Wario Ware* series are not vignettes; they do not lightly paint a sense of an experience or character; rather, they overtly depict mechanics thinly wrapped in a fictional skin. The small-scale experiences of casual puzzle games like *Zuma* are too abstract and unremitting to sketch a particular experience. When larger-scale commercial games attempt similar goals, they typically do it through narrative techniques like cinematics, as in the cutscenes of *Final Fantasy VII,* or through artifactual evidence, as in the found recordings and notebooks in *Bioshock.*

In writing and cinema, the vignette is often used to inspire empathy rather than to advance narrative. *The House on Mango Street,* Sandra Cisneros's collection of poems and stories about an adolescent Hispanic girl coming of age, offers one example.[3] In film, vignetted style can be found in Robert Altman's *Short Cuts,* which offers detailed, sordid glimpses into the lives of residents of Los Angeles.[4] The vignette is neither essay nor documentary. It does not make an argument, but characterizes an experience.

Hush offers a glimpse of how vignettes can inspire empathy in games. As an exploration of the potential of the style, the game is a success. And as a vignette of a situation in mid-1990s civil war–torn Rwanda, the game offers a compelling invitation to empathize with an actor in that geopolitical system without emphasizing the latter's operation. The anxiety of literal death contradicts the core mechanic's demand for calm in a surprising and satisfying way, like chili in chocolate. The increasingly harsh sound of a baby's cry that comes with failure attenuates the player's anxiety, further underscoring the tension at work in this grave scenario.

Perhaps in 1982 the world was not ready for a videogame about the loneliness and frailty of an extraterrestrial. But, oddly, we were ready for a film about it. *E.T.*'s role in the videogame crash has surely been overstated, but certainly players and developers alike have used its failure as part of an ongoing excuse to embrace only roles of power, and never those of weakness. Critics might argue that frail situations are not fun. Feeble characters do not wear shoes anyone wants to wear. And that may be true. But when it comes to the world we inhabit today, it is the vulnerable—like E.T., or better yet, like the Darfuris or the Rwandans—who deserve our empathy.

3

Reverence

Videogames are often accused of disrespect, especially for celebrating violence and for encouraging disdain of man, woman, and culture alike. But can a game do the opposite, embracing respect, deference, even reverence?

In 2007 the Church of England threatened to sue Sony Computer Entertainment Europe for depicting the Manchester Cathedral in its sci-fi shooter *Resistance: Fall of Man.* The church had complained about the game's inclusion of the cathedral, which was named and modeled after the seven-hundred-year-old church in this industrial city in northwest England. After considerable pressure and public condemnation, Sony issued a public apology.[1] In a statement, the company expressed regret for offending the church or the residents of Manchester, but not for including the cathedral in the game.

Amazingly, but perhaps not surprisingly, none of the mass media coverage of the cathedral controversy discusses the game itself. Sony didn't say much about it either, save a self-defeating statement from noting that the title is "a fantasy science fiction game and is not based on reality."[2] This statement implies, but does not actually address, the absurdity of critiquing a game about a hypothetical postwar twentieth century in which a hybrid alien race called the Chimera invade and assimilate the human population. But neither Sony nor the developer Insomniac Games ever tried to explain why they wished to include the cathedral in the first place. Ironically, the cathedral creates one of the most significant experiences in the whole game, one steeped in reverence for the cathedral and the church rather than desecration.

< 24 >

Resistance is not a game richly imbued with wisdom. It is a first-person shooter, and a pretty good one. It's beautifully rendered, taking apparent advantage of the advanced graphical capabilities of the PlayStation 3. The game is linear, both in its plot and the paths through each level, but that linearity allows it to focus the player on a smaller, more tightly crafted environment. *Resistance* takes up a common theme in science fiction: an ultimate test of humankind against the Other. This is also one of the classic themes of videogames, one that has been around since *Space Invaders.*

Because of its simplicity, *Resistance* is also a predictable game. You shoot aliens. A lot of them, over and over again. Your character, Sgt. Nathan Hale, is a one-note brute of a fellow with a mysterious past and a permanently furrowed brow. As is the case in most games of this kind, he is alone in his quest to rid the world of its space invaders, a turn justified by a feeble deus ex machina at the game's outset, when all of Hale's unit is killed in a series of overwhelming ambushes.

Manchester Cathedral's representatives expressed their affront in two ways.[3] The first appealed to intellectual property. They claimed that Sony did not have the right to include the cathedral's name, image, or architecture in the game in the first place.

Discussions of intellectual property rights have become so common, they risk replacing talk about the weather. Lawyers alone once obsessed over ownership, but now organizations and individuals alike invoke proprietary rights as cultural currency. The videogame industry is among the worst culprits of this practice. The public may squint when Disney lobbies to extend copyright terms to cover the products it itself adapted from public domain fairy tales, but no one bats an eye when videogame publishers issue press releases about their "all new intellectual property" or when journalists refer to forthcoming titles as "new IP" instead of "new creative work."

If a movie studio had wanted to film a scene for a postapocalyptic action film in the Manchester Cathedral, indeed it would have had to get the diocese's permission. But not for the right to depict the cathedral—that could have been done by shooting from the street outside. Rather, the film crew would have needed to get the rights to be on location, including accounting for any potential damage and covering insurance lest anyone be injured during the shoot. What if the movie studio had created a computer graphics Manchester Cathedral, shot their scene on the lot with green screens, and digitally composited the shots together? The answer is unclear, as digital rights usage for landmarks is largely untested.

The cathedral's second affront appealed to media outrage. Manchester's bishop took the opportunity to issue a statement against videogame violence in the broadest sense, connecting his objections to the city of Manchester's ongoing gun crime problem and the church's record of youth support.[4]

Let's leave the issue of property rights issues to the attorneys. Instead, consider the cultural issues. What does Manchester Cathedral mean in the game, and why might its appearance support the cathedral's relevance more than it detracts from it?

A cynic, unbeliever, or Internet troll might point out the irony of the church pointing the finger, given the millennia-old history of church-sponsored violence. A gamer might rely on the title's status as fantasy fiction to nullify the validity of the affront. Such impressions are merely instrumental attempts to foil the church's parry rather than reasoned attempts to justify the expressive ends served by depicting the cathedral in the game. And despite its creators' silence on the matter, the game does indeed have one.

Perhaps the most interesting part of *Resistance* is its depiction of repurposed spaces of 1950s Britain. The game is set on an alternate time line, but one that shares much with our own history, making its environment familiar. This feature distinguishes *Resistance* from similar games with wholly invented worlds, like *Halo*. For example, early in the game the humans make a stand at a bus depot, period-appropriate vehicles strewn asunder. Later a fish cannery becomes a breeding ground for human–alien hybrids. The military occupation of civilian spaces is the reality of any wars fought on civilian terrain, but videogames have a unique power to simulate the experience of this estrangement thanks to their propensity for world building. The first time the player cowers behind a bus or encounters a destroyed bathroom, the reality of war surfaces in a powerful way. The Manchester Cathedral level is the most powerful of these moments, and also the subtlest in this otherwise barefaced fantasy shooter.

Churches have a long history of providing alms, community, safe houses, care, and passage. The earliest hospitals were often created by bishops and other clergy to serve the local poor and sick, or travelers on pilgrimage. In the fictional backstory of *Resistance,* Manchester Cathedral had been converted for use as a hospital during the Chimera's initial attack. On entering, the player can see the rows of cots and dismantled medical equipment. Either this field hospital had been abandoned, or, more likely, its patients and staff had been overcome.

In "civilized" wars, opponents distinguish military from civilian targets. The fact that the cathedral-made-hospital was not spared attack in the game's fiction not only helps establish the savage inhumanity of the Chimera but also demonstrates that in the face of this apocalypse, the church carried out its charter, to support people in need, to stand resolved in the face of death. Some might argue that such a claim could be made about any church. In their rejoinder of Sony, the Church of England asked this very question: why Manchester instead of a fictional city?

Videogames frequently re-create real cities as settings. Usually these cities are immediately identifiable for players worldwide: Los Angeles (*True Crime: Streets of LA*), London (*The Getaway*), New York (*The Godfather*). Such major cities provide a built-in context for gameplay that helps set expectations and context. *Resistance* uses real locations but not well-known ones—Manchester, Nottingham, Bristol, York. This wasn't a matter of hometown pride; Insomniac is based in Burbank, California. Outside the UK, players likely have little or no personal experience of cities like Manchester, and thus their expectations for

geographic accuracy are lowered. Like Burbank, Manchester conjures up a culturally specific location without the overwhelming
expectation of cities known the world over.

Manchester Cathedral cements this sense of place in the game.
The cathedral is an impressive monument, a marker of cultural
and social heritage with a long history. It was constructed in the
thirteenth and fourteenth centuries, in the Gothic style common
to that era. The cathedral occupies a prominent place in central
Manchester, a historic region of the city that can trace its roots
back to the first century A.D.

Graphical realism is where PlayStation 3 really shines, and the
in-game cathedral is a convincing rendering of the real thing. As
with most Gothic churches, the player can't help but look up to
take in the sublime grandeur of the cathedral on entry. The game
affords a few seconds of exploration and awe, but then a torrent of
Chimera appears, a barrage of creatures unlike any that the player
has previously encountered in the game. The natural response is
to unleash a frenzy of fire, swirling rapidly around the cathedral,
between what remains of its pews and its enclaves. Careful cover
and selective bursts are not much of an option here.

Apocalypse films often use monuments—the White House,
the Empire State Building—as symbols for total destruction.
Indeed, the terrorist attacks of September 11, 2001, targeted
structures with symbolic as well as military and economic value.
But *Resistance* does not use Manchester Cathedral in this way.
The Chimera have no interest in destroying a monument, nor do
they have any concern for ailing, human civilians in a makeshift
church hospital. The game's detailed, accurate re-creation of the
cathedral, as well the structure's symbolic isolation in its own special level, encourages the player to pay attention to the structure.
It is not just another anonymous row house or shack or factory.
Instead, it's a structure of note, a unique place, one that demands
respect. This sense of awe stands in stark opposition to that of
the Chimera, who disrupt and undermine the cathedral's sublime

aesthetics and religious purpose. The cathedral does not become a symbol of humanity's annihilation but of the Chimera's total disregard for human culture and creativity. This is a much worse nightmare vision than simple eradication.

It is not Sony or Insomniac who defile the Manchester Cathedral in *Resistance: Fall of Man*. It is the Chimera who do. Their casual contempt for the structure cements the player's understanding of these mutant creatures as *entirely inhuman*, so much so that they aren't even capable of noticing markers of human ethos such that they might choose to destroy them outright.

Yes, the player must discharge his or her weapons inside the cathedral to avoid defeat. But when the dust settles, the cathedral empties, and the player is left to spend as much or as little time as he or she wants exploring the cathedral's cavernous interior. For it survives the barrage, much like the real Manchester Cathedral withstood a German bomb attack during World War II. Since *Resistance* is such a linear, scripted game, this open time is unusual, even excessive. It offers a break from the incessant bombardment of indistinguishable Chimera. It's a time to pause, to reflect, perhaps even to meditate on the relationship between God, human, and alien.

Manchester Cathedral was ransacked during the English Civil War in 1649, half-destroyed by a German blitz in 1940, and bombed by the Irish Republican Army in 1996. It survived all these attacks. Its patrons rebuilt it. And it still stands today. *Resistance* adds a fictional homage to the church's resolve, this time in an alternate history fought by an enemy that neither understands nor cares for human practices like religion. And it survives this as well. The Church of England sees its cathedral's presence in *Resistance* only as a sordid juxtaposition, the sanctity of worship set against the profanity of violence. But when viewed in the context of the game's fiction, the cathedral serves a purpose in the game consonant with its role in the world: that of reprieve for the weary and steadfastness in the face of devastation.

4 Music

We tend to think of music as a purely aural medium. But one need not search hard to find that listening is only one way we experience music. In the ancient world, for example, music and literature were indistinguishable. Epic poetry like that of Homer wasn't read in bound volumes but sung by minstrels who performed for groups. Shorter ancient verse, called *lyric* poetry, was so named because it was written to be sung with the accompaniment of a lyre.

From the early first millennium through the Middle Ages, music served a liturgical purpose. The plainchant (most know it better as the Gregorian chant, thanks to a compilation made by Pope Gregory the Great in the seventh century) wasn't intended to be particularly musical, but to prime the listener for spiritual reflection. By the twelfth century *jongleurs* revisited the ancient oral tradition, performing songs and tricks in the streets and courts of medieval Europe. A combination of secular and religious hymns emerged in the early Renaissance, and by the sixteenth century composers were penning music for church and concert alike. Music became more theatrical, with stagings of orchestras and, of course, opera's emergence in the seventeenth century. The melodic age of the eighteenth and nineteenth centuries saw music rise to the level of art, thanks largely to great composers like Mozart and Beethoven. Throughout this era, music still largely served a narrative or painterly purpose, whereby the music was a medium for carrying another message entirely, whether from the church, the people, or the imagination.

The twentieth century witnessed new styles, among them jazz, which secularized the sacred traditions of music and movement

< 30 >

in Africa and blended them with the instrumental and performative role of music in the West. Dance has existed throughout human history, but the last century reintroduced music as a habitat for movement and action. The Victorian waltz, the modern stadium rock concert, the 1930s swing club, the rave warehouse, all of these venues exemplify music's carnivalesque role as an invitation to overcome inhibitions and to perform physically in ways otherwise prohibited by polite society.

Music's strong social history notwithstanding, today we often use it in isolation. We insert our earbuds in the gym or on the subway as much to drown out sound as to take it in. The concert and the dance club still exist, but we've also adopted new musical functions. The emergence of soft jazz and piped music slows down and calms listeners in elevators or shopping malls, reducing anxiety during idle waiting and encouraging browsing while shopping. The music video may have been popularized by MTV in the 1980s, but it had existed in prototypical form in the silent film of the 1910s, the musical film of the early 1960s, and the promotional films of the later part of that decade. It was this latter application that most influenced the MTV generation: short films set to songs acted as advertising for singles, albums, concerts, and the musical artist more broadly. While it still serves as promotion today, the music video has exceeded this purpose, and it now acts like storytelling or vignette as much as the medieval *chanson de geste* or the early modern opera had done.

Videogames enter the domain of music here, in the era of television. While much of the history of music takes place in the public space of ritual or diversion, videogames enter the picture at a time when more and more cultural activity began to take place at home. Even as memories of Woodstock were still fresh, the idea of capturing the experience of psychedelic musical theatrics at home was already in developers' minds in the early 1970s. The year before the introduction of its seminal Video Computer System, Atari created the Atari Video Music, a hi-fi system component that could connect to a television through an RF adapter.

The device accepted RCA inputs from a stereo audio source, and then used the changing signals to modify the parameters of an abstract pattern rendered on the television—an early version of the visualizers that come with today's computer music programs like iTunes or WinAmp. Push buttons and potentiometers allowed the operator to modify the output by changing the pattern, colors, and shapes.

Like the music video or the opera, Atari Video Music made an auditory medium visual. But unlike those earlier forms, the device focused on manipulating the audio signal itself, the music directly instrumenting the visuals. The device could hardly be called interactive, but the viewer can manipulate its settings, effectively "playing along" with familiar music in an unfamiliar way.

While primitive, Atari Video Music offers a sign of what would become the unique contribution videogames offer to the experience of music. Instead of listening, watching, dancing, or otherwise taking in music, videogames offer a way to *perform* it. Naturally, one can perform music without the aid of a computer— playing the guitar or the piano or the bassoon hardly requires the aid of a videogame, nor does it constitute a novel way to experience music. But videogames offer something subtly different than playing a traditional instrument: just as Atari Video Music renders audio on a television screen in a new, unexpected way, so videogames apply a distortion to musical performance, shedding new light on seemingly familiar songs, sounds, or rhythms.

These days, the most visible sorts of videogame renditions of music are the rock performance games *Guitar Hero* and *Rock Band.* Games in these two series ask players to manipulate simplified versions of guitar, bass, drum, and vocal parts to complete songs in the context of a fictional cover band rising to the top of the charts by playing real hits from classic and modern rock. Following in the footsteps of dance games like *Dance Dance Revolution,* these games are usually categorized under the genre *rhythm action,* as they require the player to depress a particular set of buttons at the right time. For the vocal track, or in the vocals-only varieties of these games like *Singstar,* the player must sustain an accurate tone at correct intervals. Success allows song's notes and vocals to be heard through the speakers.

Thanks to the massive commercial success of music performance games, they've enjoyed a great deal of public attention, including both support and lamentation. The commonest critique surrounds the fear that "fake" instruments and cursory understanding risk replacing real engagement with musical creativity. Researchers have responded that *Guitar Hero* and its ilk do just the opposite, *culturing* a new interest in music. In a 2008 study conducted in the UK, more than half of young people reported playing music games, a fifth of whom said they took up an instrument after the videogames spurred their interest.[1]

That might very well be the case, but as the game designer Frank Lantz quips, why should we celebrate the fact that videogames might encourage teenagers to pick up the rock guitar? In twenty-five years, will we see a new trend in, say, robotics that encourages kids to play videogames?[2] Praise or blame for *Guitar Hero* should surely come from something other than its mere ability to help or hinder a kid's likelihood to play the guitar.

Here Atari Video Music's lesson is instructive. Like the hi-fi gadget that allowed its viewer to "play" a familiar song visually, making it possible literally to see music in a different way, so *Guitar Hero* and *Rock Band* do the same. But instead of recasting songs as psychedelic light shows, these music performance games abstract away the dance or lyrical quality of songs, forcing the player to focus on their rhythmic and musical construction. When you play *Guitar Hero,* you see, feel, and hear the musical patterns in a song that otherwise go unnoticed, blending into the overall flow and feel of its melody, harmonies, and rhythm. When forced to execute the notes of a run through a hammer-on or a pull-off, the abstract patterns of these playing techniques rise above the din of the song itself.

In the games, songs are grouped not by genre or period but by difficulty level, with wider variation and more rapid change in fretting, plucking, or sustaining becoming the primary organizing principles. Yet they are not mere pedagogical prototypes. The experience of playing a song again and again in *Guitar Hero* or *Rock Band,* at higher and higher levels and toward greater and greater mastery, does not lead the player to a greater state of mastery as a musician but to a greater depth of understanding as a listener.

It is here that the true aesthetics of *Guitar Hero, Rock Band, Singstar, Karaoke Revolution,* and *Dance Dance Revolution* take root: by becoming increasingly familiar with a song's structure and form, players experience the transition from the technical pedantry of an amateur to the smooth confidence of an expert. In *Dance Dance Revolution,* the expertise is not that of musical creation but of musical response: the patterns of steps, movements, and shifts out of which a dance is constructed. This ratcheting up from basics to fluency makes these games *music performance* games, not just rhythm action games. The feeling of performing comes partly from the visual and aural simulation of a crowd on the screen, and partly as a side effect of the requirement to stand up with a plastic instrument in front of friends. But even more so, the process of unlocking the songs' deep structure allows the player to experience the performance in its professional sense, through a transition from fumbling novice to effortless master.

Guitar Hero–style games offer a new perspective on musical performance by simulating the *actual* performance of music in an abstract but relatively direct way. Other possibilities exist, too. In Nintendo's *Rhythm Heaven,* a game for the Nintendo DS handheld system, the player uses the stylus to tap, flick, hold, slide, and release on the DS touchscreen in concert with the rhythm of simple compositions. In this respect, the game bears much similarity to *Dance Dance Revolution* or *Rock Band.* But *Rhythm Heaven* does away with the natural mappings between instruments and their rhythms, replacing the visuals and player interactions with arbitrary, often absurd fictional skins. To play the game, the player must operate a series of weird minigames by performing rhythmically along with a musical accompaniment.

In one such game an Easter Island mo'ai incants an abstract tune. The player, controlling the opening and closing mouth of another monolith with the stylus, must repeat the first statue's pattern correctly. In another, the player operates a fuel dispenser at a robot factory. The computer sets the parts of a robot in time with the rhythm of the music, and the player must tap and hold the stylus for the correct number of beats to fill it completely without overflowing. In yet another, the player helps a güiro lizard attract a mate by rubbing its tail against its back (through the stylus on the touch screen), which makes a noise.

Obviously, the mating habits of lizards and the songs of humanoid monoliths have little to do with the reality of music performance. But by recasting the rhythmic patterns as concrete, if fantastic actions, the game distorts the very concept of rhythm into the side effects of successful performance in comical games. The result allows the player to grasp rhythm in a different way, by wielding scratching lizard, emoting statue, eating monk, and other oddities simultaneously as actor and as instrument.

Like Atari Video Music, *Rhythm Heaven* offers a different perspective on music. By operating a device that intersects with musical performance but does not mirror it, this and other music videogames offer what the philosopher Slavoj Žižek calls a "*parallax view*," a shifting perspective between two points without synthesis.[3] Atari Video Music invites the listener to render music visible via the distorted abstractions of a circuit connected to a hi-fi system, and *Rhythm Heaven* invites the player to render music operational via the distorted abstractions of a monk or a crane or a robot fueler. It's a connection that even extends into the paratext of the game's marketing: just as music labels once used MTV videos to market their records and concerts, so Nintendo created an iTunes visualizer to advertise *Rhythm Heaven*. Instead of using a modern, computer-generated version of the psychedelic, abstract graphics of the original Atari Video Music, Nintendo's visualizer sets robots, spaceships, rice farmers, and mo'ai monoliths in rhythmic motion with your digital library of Björk, the Beatles, or Brahms. Altogether, plastic guitar, rhythm stylus, and visualizer remind us that music and games share a fundamental property: both are *playable*, offering their listeners and operators an expressive experience within the framework of melody and rhythm.

5 Pranks

In one of the many memorable moments of Ricky Gervais's BBC television series *The Office,* troublemaker Tim encases jobsworth Gareth's stapler in Jell-O.[1] Gareth is annoyed, and the viewer is amused, because both comprehend the act immediately: it's a prank.

Pranks are a type of dark humor that trace a razor's edge between amusement and injury. The risks inherent to pranks contribute to our enjoyment of them. This includes the danger of getting caught in the act or the chance that the object of the prank might become hurt or insulted. But risk also gives pranks their social power. Because he or she risks blame, the prankster affirms an amicable, if mischievous relationship to the victim. The same is true for the victim, when he or she chooses to laugh off the prank rather than to mope about it. If that victim later retaliates, its outcome counts as a playful type of social bonding, not as spite.

One form of videogame pranks arises from tricks that game developers play on their employers or publishers. Consider the hidden Easter egg. An Easter egg is a hidden message in media of all sorts, from movies to games. In software, Easter eggs are usually triggered by obscure sequences of commands, such as the ones that the flight simulator programmers hid in *Microsoft Excel 97.*

Software Easter eggs arose as a partial response to the cold anonymity of the computer, and the first videogame Easter egg had precisely this purpose in mind. In the late 1970s engineers at Atari created games singlehandedly, from concept to completion. Despite their undeniable role as authors of these games, the company did not publish credits on the box, cartridge, or manual.

< 37 >

In the absence of such official recognition, programmers some-times hid a signature within the game. When Warren Robinett completed his best-selling classic *Adventure* in 1978, he includ-ed a hidden room with graphics that read "Created by Warren Robinett."[2]

The process of discovering the hidden message was com-plex and counterintuitive, although not difficult enough that it couldn't be done (the prank was revealed when a fifteen-year-old player wrote to Atari asking about it).[3] Atari would eventually use the gag to their own benefit, spinning it as a "secret message" in the first issue of the fan magazine *Atari Age*. Soon enough, the company's higher-ups embraced the Easter egg as a way to deepen players' relationships with their titles. Howard Scott Warshaw's inclusion of his initials in 1982's *Yars' Revenge* was fully endorsed by management.

A more controversial Easter egg–style prank can be found in *SimCopter*, a 1996 Maxis title that lets players fly helicopter missions around the cities they create in *SimCity 2000*. The de-veloper Jacques Servin secretly added Speedo-clad male bimbos (Servin called them "himbos") who would meander through the city and passionately kiss.[4] In interviews Servin has cited several motivations for the prank, including gay pride (the himbos came out, so to speak, on particular dates, among them Servin's boy-friend's birthday) and poor working conditions.[5] He was subse-quently fired. This was just the start of pranking for Servin, who has since made a practice of public interventions as a member of the subversive activist collectives The Yes Men and RTMark, the latter having been the sponsor of the *SimCopter* prank.

Despite their clear status as prank, Easter eggs play jokes on games' sponsors or publishers but do not turn the games *them-selves* into pranks. To find games that play practical jokes on their players, I'll have to turn to pranks of another sort.

Many pranks function by subtlety rather than flamboyance: connecting a coworker's supply of paper clips together so they pull out of a drawer in a long chain; switching the "push" and "pull" signs on an outside door; taping over the laser eye of an optical mouse so it doesn't work; or tying someone's shoelaces together. These small-scale pranks are probably the commonest type. They don't require significant preparation, yet they can facilitate an on-going feud among participants. The setup and follow-through of small-scale tricks can even take on a playfulness that resembles a game. At the office, these activities often revolve around limited resources. One might hide or move supplies of particular worth, or plot to arrive at the office early to lock a coworker out of the best parking spaces.

Perhaps it's no surprise that these topics might translate directly into games that let players play pranks on each other, through the game itself. Take parking, a strange and complex social activity that Area/Code adapted into the Facebook game *Parking Wars*.

In *Parking Wars* each player gets a street with several spaces as well as a handful of cars, which come in different colors. Play involves the virtual parking of these cars on the simulated streets of one's Facebook friends. Each car earns money by remaining parked on the street over time, but a player can cash out a car's earned value only by moving it to another space. Players level up at specific dollar figures, earning new cars as they do so. Some spaces have special rules, like "red cars only" or "no parking allowed." It's possible to park illegally in these spaces, but if their owners catch you they can choose to issue a ticket, which tows the player from the space and forfeits the money earned to the space's owner.

When possible, it's best to park legally. This isn't easy in practice, however, since many players vie for the limited resources of their friends' collective parking lots, just like they do with coworkers at the office. And very occasionally the signs on spaces change, so safety is never guaranteed.

Playing *Parking Wars* is an exercise in predicting friends' schedules. A colleague in Europe is likely to be sleeping during the evening in the North America, and thus his street might offer safe haven at that hour. And just as some meter maids don't get around to patrolling real streets, so some players of *Parking Wars* don't get around to patrolling their virtual one. Of course, such players might just be busy, or they might even be baiting their colleagues so that they can later issue a whirlwind of unexpected tickets.

Receiving a ticket in *Parking Wars* isn't a prank on the level of spreading dog poo on the underside of a buddy's car-door handle. Rather, the combination of latent, ongoing play and occasional "gotchas" makes plays in *Parking Wars* feel like pranks. The game weaves its way into the player's ordinary use of Facebook, rather than requiring complete immersion. This latency creates a credible context for surprises, just as the flow of the workday sets the stage for switched desk drawers or shoe polish–smeared telephone receivers. Gotchas come in at least two forms: in giving or receiving a ticket (which pops up as a big, bright overlay across the screen), and in the silent knowledge of having taken advantage of another player's inattention.

Many games give players the opportunity to trick, fool, or swindle an opponent out of resources—just recall the pleasure of seeing an opponent land on a particularly valuable property in Monopoly. But in *Parking Wars* players aren't always expecting it. By setting up an ordinary social environment for disruption, *Parking Wars* becomes a medium for pranks, a kind of videogame whoopee cushion.

The parking space reminds us that the office is a popular venue for pranks. We're stuck there most of the day, everyday, by necessity more than by choice. Moreover, we have little if any control over our fates during the workday; the worker's time is supposed to be spent at labor, efficiently producing widgets or moving information. We prank at work to exert agency in an otherwise uncontrollable environment. As with Robinett's Easter egg, office pranks help their perpetrators exert their humanity in an age of industry. But even more so, pranks offer an opportunity to undermine the very values of the office.

Consider again the world of *The Office*. A prank like Tim's in the show's first episode brings us pleasure because it requires an involved setup that cashes out in only a few moments of amusement. It also amuses us because we can imagine all the work Gareth has to do to retrieve his stapler—unearthing it from the jelly mound, soaking it in hot water to remove the excess. Other pranks on this scale include covering someone's entire office in aluminum foil, or drywalling over the boss's door, or filling a coworker's cubicle with packing peanuts. The workers depicted in the television show push paper in two ways: first in the usual sense of mindless tasks, and second in the literal peddling of office paper, the business of the show's fictional company. The jelly-bound stapler draws our attention to the blind pushing of papers and sets the stage for the social critique that follows in subsequent episodes. The prank is what the show is about.

Historically, there are many examples of pranks as confrontational responses to social and cultural situations. The Dadaists embraced anti-art like the nonsense poetry of Tristan Tzara and the found art of Marcel Duchamp. Just as Tim's jelly stapler undermines the logic of work, so Dada pranks the rationalist ideals of West. In the 1950s the beat concept of the Happening popularized public performance art, a concept the situationists made political in the 1960s. The "situation" used public performance to critique the foundations of everyday life on which it relied. Situations helped lay the cultural groundwork for more recent public pranks like flash mobs, which often draw attention to how public space has become privatized or monitored. Pranks like situations and flash mobs first amuse, or distract, or disturb just like any other gag. But they also dig deep into social conventions, laying them bare in mockery and reclaiming them in liberation. Television offers a more contemporary example: parodies like *The Daily Show* and *The Colbert Report* prank broadcast shows to undermine those show's pretenses, absconding with their audiences along the way.

Some games attempt to direct similar ridicule at the very conventions of gameplay. One is Myfanwy Ashmore's *Mario Battle No. 1*, a hack of the *Super Mario Bros.* Nintendo Entertainment System cartridge in which all platforms, enemies, and objects have been removed, resulting in an empty expanse with no goals and no challenges. When time runs out, Mario dies. By laying the architecture of the game bare, *Mario Battle No. 1* invites the player to ask deeper questions in their absence: where do the Goombas come from? Do they serve Bowser willingly?

But like Cory Arcangel's *Super Mario Clouds*, *Mario Battle No. 1* is more art object than videogame prank; it is not really playable as a game, at least in the same way *The Daily Show* is viewable as television.[6] A better example of a game convention prank is *Syobon Action* (*Dejected Action*), a Japanese platformer also known in the West as "*Cat-Mario*" or simply "Mario from Hell." The game is playable, challenging, and enjoyable, but it is constructed in a way that defies every expectation of Mario-style platform conventions.

In *Syobon Action,* the floor sometimes falls away unexpectedly. An invisible coin-box appears as the player attempts to jump a chasm, hurtling him or her down into it instead. A bullet fires from an unseen source off-screen just in time to knock the player from the most direct trajectory across an obstacle. Hidden blocks trap the player if he or she doesn't take a counterintuitive path. Spikes randomly extrude from some surfaces after the player steps on them.

The game's genius is that of a well-honed, methodically planned prank: it systematically disrupts every expected convention of 2-D platform gameplay. Instead of allowing equal viability to numerous approaches to a physical challenge, the game demands that the player undertake bizarre and arbitrary routes. It punishes rather than rewards genre conventions, like item collection (in addition to coins and power-ups, enemies sometimes pop out of question-mark blocks). And the rules change arbitrarily: sometimes a mushroom acts as a power-up, other times it turns the player into a robot that crashes through the floor and dies. The game takes control away from the player and uses carefully timed trickery to make decisions that would be reasonable in the original game require complete rethinking.

For example, the game preserves the end-level flagpole familiar to *Super Mario Bros.* fans but distorts it perversely. Just as the player jumps off the ledge toward the flagpole, a long projectile streaks across the screen; the only way to avoid it is to backtrack onto the ledge again to jump over it. After successfully mounting the flagpole, the game takes control of the player character and moves it toward the castle, just as in *Super Mario Bros.* But a carefully timed enemy falls from the sky, colliding with and killing the player. Success comes only when the player jumps over the flagpole, avoids the resulting enemy, and then backtracks to complete the level.

Complex pranks like the jelly stapler, the foil-wrapped office, and the unconventional platformer are amusing when witnessed and annoying when experienced. But they also act as profound social interventions. By mocking the rules we don't otherwise question, they possess carnivalesque qualities; they allow us to suspend our ordinary lives and to look at them from a different perspective. It's possible to pass *Syobon Action* off on a friend as a legitimate Mario clone, only to laugh uproariously when things start to go wrong. This is the garlic-flavored gum usage of the game. But it's also possible to let *Syobon Action* prank you willingly, as a player, to stop and reflect on the conventions of platform play that have become so familiar that they seem second nature. Just as Tim's stapler gag mocks the values of office productivity, so *Syobon Action* indicts the specialized language of videogame geekery. This is the Dadaist usage of the game.

As videogames become a larger part of everyday life, the opportunities to prank friends, coworkers, housemates, and family members in videogame form will surely increase. But part of the momentum required to carry out a prank is in its customization. *Parking Wars* is a commercial effort, funded by A&E as an advergame to promote a television series of the same name. But *Syobon Action* is an independent title, a curiosity produced for its own sake and at great effort. The future of videogame pranks relies on several literacies that are not yet well developed. Videogame pranksters must have the know-how to make games and to integrate prankish ideas into them, or to manipulate the contexts for existing games to transform them into pranks. A much deeper fluency with game conventions, tools, and craft will be required for videogame pranks to become an ongoing concern. They are commercially unviable in large part, but socially meaningful, justifying considerable effort even if they disappear soon after use, like the Jell-O that melts when Gareth retrieves his stapler.

6
Transit

Automobile manufacturers and airlines sometimes try to hawk their wares by suggesting "the journey is half the fun." In today's world of low-frills, high-speed transportation, it's a tough pill to swallow. But there was a time when one had no choice but to think of the journey as part of the trip, simply because it took so long to get anywhere.

In the mid-eighteenth century, for example, it would have taken ten days to travel from London to Edinburgh by horse and carriage under the best conditions.[1] By the 1830s the trip took less than two days by railroad. The convenience, speed, and economy of rail travel were immediately apparent for both freight and transit purposes, and the early days of rail made it clear that the new technology had fundamentally changed the very experience of travel.

While the railroad introduced many changes, two stand out from the perspective of tourism. First, by removing the majority of time from a journey, the railroad also removed much of the experience of the space traversed. Even though travelers covered the same distance, the new speed by which one would pass that expanse made it impossible to experience space in the same way. In his history of the railway journey, Wolfgang Schivelbusch describes it as follows:

> On the one hand, the railroad opened up new spaces that were not as easily accessible before; on the other, it did so by destroying space, namely the space between points. That in-between, or travel space, which it was possible to

< 45 >

"savor" while using the slow, work-intensive eotechnical form of transport, disappeared on the railroads.[2]

Schivelbusch compares this change with the "loss of aura" in mechanically produced works of art, as famously theorized by Walter Benjamin.[3] While waypoints along a route had once been connected to one another continuously through the slow traversal of foot, horse, or carriage, the railroad disrupted this uninterrupted flow. As Schivelbusch explains, "What was experienced as being annihilated was the traditional space-time continuum which characterized the old transportation technology. Organically embedded in nature as it was, that technology, in its mimetic relationship to the space traversed, permitted the traveler to perceive that space as a living entity."[4]

Second, the railroad changed the traveler's experience of the countryside as it was seen from the railcar. The carriage or horseback had provided a relatively unmediated view of the passing landscape. If the traveler so wished, he or she could interrupt a journey and step down from the coach to inspect a vista or to meander into a meadow. But even from his or her seat, the traveler experienced a more deliberate revealing of scenes along the route. That changed with the railroad, which bombarded ever forward, along the single path afforded by the iron road, each particular scene visible through the railcar's window for only a brief moment. If the carriage functioned more like a landscape painting, the railway functioned like a cinema camera. Schivelbusch explains:

The empirical reality that made the landscape seen from the train window appear to be "another world" was the railroad itself, with its excavations, tunnels, etc. Yet the railroad was merely an expression of the rail's technological requirements, and the rail itself was a constituent part of the machine ensemble that was the system. It was, in other words, that machine ensemble that interjected itself between the traveler and the landscape. The traveler perceived the landscape as it was filtered through the machine ensemble.[5]

Schivelbusch's thoughts about the railroad remind us that travel is not a universal experience but one mediated by the particular forms that give rise to it. A continuous, sensory voyage through slowly transforming countryside characterized travel by carriage. In the age of rail, the train produced a staccato vista through its single view. And of course today, in the era of the airplane, the vistas of travel have been removed entirely, replaced by the white blanket of clouds or the vague pattern of farmland five miles below. In a practice begun thanks to the railway, travelers now replace the landscape traveled with the "imaginary, surrogate landscape" of the book—a form that enjoyed considerable success when sold or loaned in rail stations.[6]

In the century preceding the rise of the rail, media had already begun to offer a kind of practice run for the travel experience to come. In "panorama" shows, audiences viewed paintings of distant destinations without requiring the massive time and expense necessary for a journey abroad. Schivelbusch recounts such a scene:

A newspaper of the year 1843 describes the Parisian public "reclining on well-upholstered seats and letting the five continents roll by at its pleasure without having to leave the city and without having to risk bad weather, thirst, hunger, cold, heat, or any danger whatsoever."[7]

The railroad soon offered a real implementation of the panorama, a summary view of the countryside. But the panorama show foreshadowed the coming railroad age, offering an early taste of something that was still impossible at the time.

If the panorama anticipated a kind of travel yet to come, the videogame looks back on one that's already passed. Games restore the experience of resistance and adventure that the rail (and the airplane after it) had removed from travel, even if only through simulation.

For one part, a videogame constantly asks its players to *act*. The seemingly passive experience of piloting a car around *Grand Theft Auto*'s Liberty City becomes a task in the game's larger mobster fiction. And in many games, including the characteristically forgettable ones that adapt motion pictures, a story's plot is mapped to the physical traversal of a landscape, such that solving a problem amounts to moving successfully through the obstacles of an environment.

But for another part, videogames tend to offer continuous rather than discontinuous space that must be traversed deliberately and actively, the opposite of the panorama show and the railway. Even the earliest 2-D games rely on patient traversal as fundamentals: the spaceship of *Asteroids* moving through its field of rocks, Pac-Man moving through his maze collecting pellets. But it's 3-D games that make continuous transit a fundamental part of the experience of play.

Crazy Taxi was first created for coin-op play, but was popularized with its release on the Sega Dreamcast in 2000. The game plays just like its title suggests: the player takes the role of a cabbie who must pick up and drop off fares at locations throughout a city. A large, green arrow at the top of the screen points the player in the general direction of the destination, but the challenge comes in navigating the winding streets of the city and countryside to reach it before the fare grows impatient.

A taxi-style minigame mimicking *Crazy Taxi* appears in *Grand Theft Auto 3*, but that title also makes transit a fundamental part of the gameplay, by situating its challenges throughout a large city that takes considerable time to traverse. *GTA3* and its sequels also offer an important shift away from the arcade-style play of *Crazy Taxi*: since players can complete missions at a time of their choosing, the game's default state is essentially that of transit. Despite popular opinions suggesting that *GTA3* allows a player to "do anything," it actually offers precious little freedom of action, since indeed only a small number of acts are really supported in the game world. Instead, the game offers freedom of continuous movement, which players sometimes partake of as its own pleasure. While the railroad cuts out the scenery and replaces it with panorama, *Grand Theft Auto* and other open-world games inspired by its design offer scenery worthy of experience in its own right.

One can walk instead of driving in *GTA*, although it's a time-consuming process. But walking also finds more fundamental integration into games in which slow, continuous traversal becomes a fundamental aspect of gameplay. In Nintendo's *Animal Crossing* series, several human players share an idyllic pastoral village with cartoonish animals. It's a strange game with few defined goals. Players can talk to the animals, fish or catch insects, search for buried treasure, buy and sell goods, and tend to the village's gardening needs. Play proceeds over many weeks or months, and the environment changes along with the calendar and the seasons.

In the process, one has to traverse the hills and paths and bridges and riverbanks of the village many, many times. Bitty the hippo might ask the player to deliver a modern table to Aziz across town, requiring the slow, pleasant promenade across the river and up the hill to the peach tree orchard on the opposite end of the village. Once there, as happenstance would often have it, Aziz might be out meandering or shopping or fishing, forcing the player to return another day to complete the errand. In the process, not just once but over many such encounters, the player develops an intuitive and continuous relationship with the village's landscape. *Grand Theft Auto* and *Crazy Taxi* simulate an experience many of us have every day: commuting by car. But *Animal Crossing* offers a surrogate for one that we began replacing first with the railroad and then with the automobile: an experience of the "space between points" that had been reduced or eliminated by the transportation technologies that began with the railroad.

One might observe that a videogame is a strange way to get a sense of the space between points when one could simply find a local park or just go outside and walk around the neighborhood. Videogames, after all, are often accused of ripping people out of the natural world and placing them into an artificial one. But this objection misses an important feature of the prerailroad transit experience: the necessary unfamiliarity of a space being traversed. Places once felt isolated from one another, and the process of traveling *itself* served to unite them. Before the railroad, the traveler also doubled as adventurer, taming the spaces in between destinations by passing through them, both literally via foot or horse or carriage and figuratively by vision and judgment. The former gets you from place to place, but the latter solidifies the continuous space of transit and the real effort required to get there.

If this distance comprises the aura lost when transportation technologies allow travelers to access a faraway locale without going through the effort of long-distance travel, then it might be tempting to see the rapidly loadable locales of *Grand Theft Auto* and *Animal Crossing* as similarly collapsed, the television and videogame console taking the place of the locomotive or the airplane. But even as these simulated places may not embrace *real* remoteness by remaining so easy to access, once there players experience a new, *simulated* remoteness: how to get from Gerry's place to the Liberty City Ferry terminal or how to find the village museum from the seashore. For these locations to simulate remoteness effectively, they must start out entirely unfamiliar, inviting the player to come to understand them through slow transit rather than the speed of transportation technologies. It helps that the temporal expectations in videogames are distorted. It might take hours to drive from Brooklyn to Hoboken, but since the action in most videogames is expected to be nearly immediate, even a small prolonging of the simulated experience reproduces the extended travel associated with earlier forms of transit.

The result inverts the function of the photograph and the panorama show in the mid-nineteenth century. Instead of looking forward to a future in which the risky, laborious process of traversing space could be lessened, in-videogame transit re-creates a past in which reality had not yet been dissolved into bits, but had to be traversed deliberately. Like the panorama show, the transit simulation is a kind of replacement therapy for an inaccessible experience of movement. Two centuries ago, that missing experience was able to truncate space. Today, it takes the reverse form, an experience that demands continuity. In this respect, the videogame is to the airplane and automobile what the on-board novel once was to the railroad.

Perhaps the most ironic example of videogame transit comes in the very simulation of the technology that first dissolved reality, the railroad itself. Games like *Microsoft Train Simulator* offer an equivalent of flight simulators for the railways. Popular mostly among railroad hobbyists, they're complex and intricate simulations of the operation of various rail lines all around the world. These titles require players to stop and start a locomotive using simulated control levers, to couple and uncouple wagons, and most of all to follow the signals and schedules necessary to deliver passengers or cargo along real or fictional routes built into the game, or constructed by the player.

From the perspective of transit simulation, perspective becomes the key feature of *Train Simulator*. Rather than being situated in the passenger carriage, where vistas captured like photographs occasionally interrupt the pleasant silence of a book, the player is thrust into the operator's cab. There, he or she not only must negotiate the physics of track curves and locomotive speeds or the symbologies of signal direction but also must embrace a continuous attention to the unfolding scene. In this case, the journey is not just half the fun but the entire experience.

7 Branding

Monopoly has a long, complex, and generally unknown history. Perhaps the most surprising detail about this classic game about being a real estate tycoon is that it was originally created with an entirely different set of values in mind.

In 1903—thirty years before the initial release of Monopoly as we know it, Elizabeth Magie Phillips designed The Landlord's Game, a board game that aimed to teach and promote Georgism, an economic philosophy that claims land cannot be owned but belongs to everyone equally. Henry George, after whom the philosophy is named, was a nineteenth-century political economist who argued that industrial and real estate monopolists profit unjustly from both land appreciation and rising rents. To remedy this problem, he proposed a "single tax" on landowners.

The Landlord's Game was intended to demonstrate how easy it is for property owners to inflict financial ruin on tenants. As a learning game and a game with a message, the title begins to look a lot more like political propaganda than entertainment. And even if Monopoly was created to celebrate rather than lament land monopolies, the game does demonstrate the landlord's power, for better or worse.

But more recently this famous game has associated itself with another side of industrial capitalism: advertising. In 2006 Hasbro released a version of Monopoly called Monopoly Here & Now. This edition offers several updates to the classic 1930s edition, including changing the properties to more widely recognizable ones: Boardwalk becomes Times Square, Park Place becomes Fenway Park.[1] Instead of paying luxury tax, the player shells out

< 52 >

for credit card debt. Cell phone services depose the electric company. Airports replace railways. And in Here & Now, you collect $2 million for passing Go. Times have changed.

Renaming properties on a Monopoly board is certainly nothing new; dozens of official and unofficial "affinity" editions of the game have been created, one for every city, college, TV show, and pastime imaginable (there's even a NASCAR edition). But Here & Now also replaces the classic game tokens with new, branded tokens. No more thimble, no more car to argue over. Instead, players can choose a Toyota Prius, McDonald's french fries, a New Balance running shoe, a Starbucks coffee mug, and a Motorola Razr phone. In addition to the branded tokens, the game includes a generic unbranded laptop, airplane, and dog.

In his book *Monopoly: The World's Most Famous Game,* Philip Orbanes details multiple versions of the game's early retail edition.[2] The familiar metal tokens had been modeled after charm bracelets, but they added to the game's cost. During the Great Depression entertainment was a luxury, and Parker Brothers also offered a less fancy version that left out the tokens to lower the product's cost. Players provided their own game tokens, often scrounging for objects of the right size and heft to use on the board. The game pieces we take for granted thus represent important aspects both of the game's historical origin (charm bracelets of the 1930s) and of its history (the financial pressures that motivated the lower-cost edition).

It might be tempting to dismiss Hasbro's move to brand these tokens as deliberately opportunistic and destructive. After all, Monopoly's branded tokens seem very similar to static in-game advertising in videogames (the sort that inserts a Honda Element on the snowboard courses in *SSX3*). Indeed, in a *New York Times* article about the new edition of Monopoly, the executive director of a consumer nonprofit did just that, calling the new edition "a giant advertisement" and criticizing Hasbro for taking "this low road."[3]

But perhaps the historical relationship between the tokens and the game's cultural origins should dampen our reaction to the little metal fries and hybrid cars. None of the brands sought out the advertising or paid a placement fee for it. Instead, Hasbro itself solicited those particular brands to appear in the game. The company's senior vice president Mark Blecher claimed that the branded tokens offer "a representation of America in the 21st century."[4] The company, argues Blecher, brings the "iconography" of commercial products to Monopoly.

Blecher is a marketing executive, so we should think twice before taking his justifications as wholesome design values. Certainly other advertising-free design choices would have been possible. The game's original tokens were jewelry sized, so perhaps a more appropriate contemporary update of small tokens would have been SD memory cards or Bluetooth earpieces.

But Blecher has a point: for better or worse, branded products are as fundamental to contemporary life as bracelet charms were in the Depression. They are the trifles, the collectibles that most of the contemporary populace uses to accessorize their lives. Here & Now uses branded tokens to define its game world as that of contemporary corporate culture, in contrast to the developer baron world of the original game.

Monopoly Here & Now bears a lesson about advertising's role in commercial videogames. Most developers are concerned with the appropriateness of brands in games, and even large publishers have shown their unwillingness to hawk in-game space even at high premiums—for example, Electronic Arts canceled its plans to sell brand placement in *The Sims 2* after failed experiments with Intel and McDonald's in *The Sims Online*.[5] Yet some developers and players also believe that branding is appropriate when it enhances realism in a game. This principle is usually cited in reference to urban and sports environments, which are littered with advertising in the real world.

In cases like these, realism usually implies *visual authenticity*— correct appearances. But Monopoly Here & Now doesn't include brands for the sake of appearance—just about any icon would have looked fine as a player token. Instead, it includes the brands to add contemporary social values to the game. Such a feat cannot be accomplished by branding alone.

In addition to promotion, in-game ads and product placements also carry the cultural payload of the brands that mark them. The result is different from visual authenticity—after all, it doesn't really matter much whether virtual billboards and sports arenas carry real ads or fake ones, so long as they look credible. Instead, advertising in games can service an authenticity of practice. Brands are built around values, aspirations, experiences, history, and ideas. Consumers make associations with brands when both are put together in particular contexts.

We might lament the prominence of material consumption in culture, but that prominence is also undeniable. No matter one's perspective on the state of capitalism today, games have not yet made much use of branding as a cultural concept. I tried to use branding for social commentary in *Disaffected!*, my videogame critique of Kinko's that uses the chain's brand reputation for rotten customer service in a satirical commentary. And Molleindustria's *McDonald's Videogame* uses that company's brand reputation for massive worldwide industrialization to expose the social dangers of global fast food. The branding in these games is unauthorized; the games critique rather than promote these companies.[6]

Of course, unauthorized brand abuse in large commercial games might not be possible or desirable. But brands' cultural values offer a bridge between visual appearance and game mechanics. In some cases, our understanding of particular rules of interaction in the world has become bonded to products and services. In a game, the behavior of a character, situation, or idea changes when aspects of that behavior can be offloaded from the simulation into a branded product or service. For example, what can you infer about a person who drives a Mitsubishi Lancer or wears Manolo Blahnik shoes? Indeed, branding strategy has been the primary method by which brands made their way into games. In auto racing games like *Gran Turismo* or flying games like *Microsoft Flight Simulator*, specific vehicle brands contribute to players' expectations when they get behind the wheel or the yoke.

This doesn't pertain just to "lovemarks," the term the ad executive Kevin Roberts has given to brands people grow to love rather than just recognize (Apple, Starbucks, and Lego are examples).[7] It also applies to less desirable brands that still convey social values—Edsel, Betamax, and Pan Am, for example. Historical brands that have passed their prime still carry extremely complicated cultural currency. For those old enough to remember them, very complex cultural and historical moments are bound up in brands like LA Gear, Hypercolor, or Ocean Pacific.

For a very different example of in-game branding as cultural currency, consider Barack Obama's 2008 campaign ads.[8] Thanks to an enormous war chest, the Obama campaign chose to experiment with nontraditional forms of advertising in addition to flooding the airwaves with television spots. One of the campaign's more unusual investments involved buying dynamic in-game advertisements in several popular console videogames. These ads are streamed into disc-based games played on an Xbox 360 or PlayStation 3 with an Internet connection, and they typically fill billboards and other simulated advertisements in games set in real-world locations. In Obama's case, the campaign focused on sports and racing titles, including *Burnout: Paradise*, an auto racing game, and *Madden '09*, the popular football game. The result was red, white, and blue, Obama-emblazoned ads skirting racetracks and stadiums, bearing appeals to vote.

The feat made Obama the first presidential candidate to advertise inside a videogame.[9] It's impossible to know if the advertisements themselves were effective at getting out the vote. But it might not matter. Monopoly Here & Now uses the Prius car and Motorola phone to inject the experience of contemporary life into the game. But Obama's ads do the opposite: they inject the experience of videogames into contemporary life. Because of its novelty, the player would likely be struck by an Obama ad in a bout of simulated basketball or hockey.

Such an ad says nothing about the candidate's qualifications or platform, of course, but it's not meant to do so. Instead, the Obama spots borrow the contemporary, technical, and computational aura of the videogame and apply them to the candidate. When combined with Obama's well-documented love for his Blackberry and his opponent John McCain's well-documented technical ineptness, buying in-game advertisements made the former candidate appear savvy, current, and young.[10] In a campaign that ran on the very concept of "change," Obama had much to gain by importing the abstract values of videogames into his image. Rather than apply Obama branding in the game, this was a case of the game branding Obama.

If we think of brands as markers for complex social behavior, we can also imagine recombining brands' encapsulated social values in new contexts: the Yugo stagecoach, or Preparation H for blood elves. These are silly examples—and some commercial developers might fear that they represent in-game advertising's worst threat: the colonization of even the most incompatible games. But as Monopoly Here & Now makes clear, advertisements contain more than just messages meant to move products on shelves. In addition, advertising encapsulates the rules of cultural preconceptions. When familiar products and services find their way into a game world, they serve as shorthand for its social and cultural circumstances. And as Obama's in-game advertisements show, the features of games also feed back on cultural circumstances themselves.

8
Electioneering

Election strategy games have been around since 1981's *President Elect,* but that title and its progeny were games about the political process, not games used as a part of that process. The 2004 election marked a turning point, however, with the birth and quick rise of the official political videogame. It was the year candidates and campaign organizations got into games, using the medium for publicity, fund-raising, platform communication, and more. That year, I worked on games commissioned by candidates for president and for state legislature, by a political party, and by a Hill committee. And that was just me—other endorsed political games abounded, from the Republican Party to the campaign for president of Uruguay.

It was easy to get public attention around such work, and indeed at the time, one benefit of campaign games revolved around their press-worthiness. By the final weeks of the 2004 election cycle, all signals suggested that campaign games were here to stay. Drunk on such videogame election elation, I remember making a prediction in a press interview that year: in 2008, I foolishly divined, every major candidate would have their own PlayStation 3 game. The MSNBC writer Tom Loftus made a similar, albeit wisely milder prediction in late October 2004: "Already tired of hearing politicians say 'visit my Web site' every five minutes? Wait until 2008, when that stump speech staple may be replaced with a new candidates' call: 'Play my game.'"[1]

We couldn't have been more wrong. Videogames played a minor role in the U.S. 2008 election (and no role whatsoever in the midterm elections of 2010). In terms of officially created or endorsed

< 58 >

work, only a few examples appeared in 2008. The McCain campaign served up *Pork Invaders,* a *Space Invaders* clone in which a McCain "ship" fires vetoes at pig "aliens" as a demonstration of how McCain "would exercise the veto pen to restore fiscal responsibility to our federal government." The game boasts higher production value than the GOP's similar 2004 offering, *Tax Invaders,* but considerably less-sophisticated political speech. *Tax Invaders* casts taxes in the role of the alien enemy and George W. Bush as the executive-hero who would save the people from them, an apt characterization of conservative tax policy that actually benefits from having been set in a videogame. By contrast, *Pork Invaders* struggles to connect gameplay to political message; it's mostly a curiosity.

The most visible videogame politicking of 2008 came in the form of advertising rather than gameplay: the Obama campaign bought dynamic in-game ads in console games like *Burnout Paradise.* Gamers welcomed the buy; it appeared to suggest that Obama at least did not intend to vilify their medium, despite having previously encouraged parents to "turn off the television set, and put the video games away."[2] Given Obama's enormous war chest, the move must have looked like a risk-free experiment to the campaign. Still, the Democrats didn't make any games of their own, a feat met (even if barely) by McCain's hammy offering.

Unofficial political games have also made few advances since 2004. The largest crop of them are gamelike gags about Sarah Palin, from the almost-topical *Polar Palin* to the toylike *Palin as President* to the wildlife send-up *Hunting with Palin* to a series of Palin chatterbots to the inevitable whack-a-mole clone *Puck Palin.* The few non-Palin titles included a retooling of 2004's derivative *White House Joust*; *Truth Invaders,* another *Space Invaders* clone in which the player shoots down lies; *Debate Night,* a Zuma-style casual game in support of Obama; and *Campaign Rush,* a click-management election office game my studio developed for CNN International. Of these, only *Truth Invaders* cites actual candidate claims and attempts to refute them, although in a fairly rudimentary way. The others do not engage policy issues at all, only electioneering. Three decades after its coin-op release, it's disillusioning to realize that *Space Invaders* has become the gold standard for political game design.

The turnout for commercial games with political themes has also thinned since the highs of 2004. That year, no less than four different election simulation games were released; but in 2008, the only offering was Stardock's retooled and updated version of *The Political Machine,* an election sim for PCs that also got a free web release that year. Beyond that, the strongest example of a mainstream game coupled to the election season is the "political brawler" *Hail to the Chimp,* a collection of party games about animals competing for the highest office in the animal kingdom.

There are reasons games have grown slowly compared with other technologies for political outreach. The most important one is also the most obvious: by 2008 online video and social networks had become the big thing, as blogs had been in 2004. Instead of urging voters to "play my game," as Loftus and I surmised, candidates urged their constituents to "watch my video." Online video became the political totem of 2008, from James Kotecki's dorm room interviews to CNN's YouTube debates. At the same time, the massive growth in social network subscriptions made social connectivity a secondary focus for campaign innovation, especially since Facebook had opened its pages beyond the campus in 2006. In many cases, politicking on social networks was a process driven entirely by voters rather than campaigns, efforts that reached far larger numbers than might have been possible previously, even with blogs.

For once, videogames did not lose an election by sticking their collective necks out as a sacrifice for values politics, the kind that Hillary Clinton and Joe Lieberman, among others, have used to shift their base toward the center. Instead, videogames lost the election by not participating in it. Precedent aside, reskinning classic arcade games and placing billboards in virtual racetracks doesn't take advantage of the potential games have to offer to political speech.

To understand why, we need to comprehend the difference between politics and politicking. *Politicking* refers to campaigning, the process we see and hear about throughout the election cycle: the yard signs, the television ads, the soapboxing, even the debates. *Politicking* is meant to get smiling faces and simple ideas in front of voters to appeal to what ails them. *Politics,* if we take the word seriously, refers to the actual executive and legislative efforts of our elected officials to alter and update the rules of our society. In an ideal representative democracy, the one leads to the other, but in contemporary society the two are orthogonal.

Ironically, this is exactly where videogames find their most natural connection to political speech. When we make videogames, we construct simulated worlds in which different rules apply. To play games involves taking on roles in those worlds, making decisions within the constraints they impose, and then forming judgments about living in them. Videogames can synthesize the raw materials of civic life and help us pose the fundamental political question, *What should be the rules by which we live?* Such questions are rarely posed or answered seriously in elections. Indeed, the electoral process has become divorced from establishing and enforcing public policy.

For a view of how this alternative might be explored through videogames, we have to travel back in time to 2004. That year, my studio worked on *Take Back Illinois,* a four-part strategy game that challenged players to play through key issues facing Illinois voters in that year's state legislative election. On the one hand, the game was very much an election game, commissioned by Tom Cross and the Illinois House Republican Organization. But on the other hand, the game focused on policy issues instead of campaign personalities.

Each of the four minigames that make up *Take Back Illinois* deals with a different issue, and one launched every week for the month before the election. The issues include medical malpractice reform, education, citizen participation, and economic reform. While still simplified compared with the operation of real public policy, the games focus on the state party's perspective on the issues rather than on the candidates (who never appear in the game). The game orients voters toward candidate and party platform positions on the issues that might affect their lives, rather than the politicians who might advance such positions.

In the case of *Take Back Illinois*, players were asked to make abstracted policy decisions and to consider their consequences. Players provided health care to a community, moving citizens to health centers and adjusting medical malpractice policy to attract or repel medical expertise; they attempted to balance the educational needs of multiple school districts to improve their effectiveness with limited resources; they attempted to inspire civic engagement by communicating the responsibility of democracy as participation; and they tried to support rural and blue-collar economic development by creating and distributing incentives for business activities and support for new job training in non-urban areas.

Take Back Illinois is not a perfect game; after all, it still operated primarily as an electioneering title, one released strategically just before the election to drive votes in local elections. But precisely because it straddles the fence between politicking and politics, it offers a compelling signal for the future role of videogames in politics. Party lines fall quite differently at the local versus the national level. While national debates swirl around values issues like family values, and while politicians and the media continue to call abstractly for an end to partisan politics, the local issues that really affect ordinary people's lives get decided behind closed doors. If the political climate demands more refined, subtle thinking about policy instead of politics, then perhaps we can imagine a future in which videogames that simulate policy positions slowly eat away at the popularity of politicking, introducing players to issues as they become relevant rather than when the election cycle necessitates it.

The solution to the failures of 2008 and 2010 is not to try again in 2012; indeed, the best solution may be to abandon the "election game" entirely, in favor of the public policy game. What if you could live a mirror life in the evolving world of your U.S. senator or city councilor's policy promotions: How would a community benefit from a bond measure in relation to its actual cost to taxpayers? What would it feel like to live under the constraints of a particular fiscal policy? How might an unorthodox energy policy balance environmental and security concerns? Why will federal investment in private banking positively affect business and ordinary citizens?

In other words, the benefit videogames can offer public life is to de-emphasize politicking in favor of policy. The role of videogames in politics lies here, in their potential to unseat elections as the unit of popular political currency, rather than to participate in them directly.

9 Promotion

In late 2006 Burger King released three Xbox and Xbox 360 titles featuring the creepy King mascot that's graced the company's advertising in recent years, as well as memorable former spoke-screatures like the Subservient Chicken and Brooke Burke. The titles include *Pocketbike Racer,* a Mario Kart–style battle racer; *Big Bumpin',* a collection of head-to-head bumper car games including races, battles, and hockey; and *Sneak King,* a stealth action game in which the player must sneak up on people and serve them Burger King foods (points are awarded for sneaking with "vigor, finesse, and a royal flourish"). To get the games, Burger King customers had to buy a Value Meal and then pay another $3.99 for each title (it was possible to buy all three with only one meal purchase).

There are several ways advertising and games intersect. One is the *advergame,* a custom-developed title, usually played on a web page, built from the ground up to promote a product or service. Another is *product placement,* the insertion of branding or products into commercial games, a technique discussed in chapter 7 in the context of *Monopoly.* And a third is *in-game advertising,* the static (fixed at development time) or dynamic (delivered over the Internet) insertion of billboards, objects, or videos into commercial titles.

Despite increases in both product placement and in-game advertising, web-based advergames remain far more common examples. The main reason for this popularity is the relatively low cost and complexity of creating branded browser-based games.

< 64 >

Since the commercialization of the Web in the mid-1990s, the vast majority of advergames have been web-based affairs, most often small casual games on corporate websites that add branding to proven genres. At first blush, the Burger King Xbox 360 games would appear to fall in the advergame tradition; like their simpler, cheaper cousins, these games build branding atop proven, popular game genres: *Pocketbike Racer* clearly arises from the now-familiar genre of go-cart racers, and *Big Bumpin'* borrows its gameplay from that same genre's head-to-head combat modes.

Yet Burger King rejects the advergaming label. As the columnist Stephen Totilo reported, Burger King promotions director Martha Tomas Flynn said the project "very much wasn't an advergaming initiative."[1] Instead, she explained, "the plan for the game[s] and where we ended up was to make a legitimate entertainment experience that uses the Burger King icons as licensed characters."

Flynn's reluctance may arise from the negative reputation advergames have earned, thanks to an overly opportunistic advertising industry that has delivered poor-quality games. Yet the Burger King games can't be accused of amateurism; they were created by UK-based Blitz Games, which has a long history of developing games based on licensed properties. Burger King and Xbox conceived the deal and brought the developers on board several months later, presumably based on their considerable experience working with licenses like *American Idol* and Bratz.

Tomas Flynn's rhetoric is an increasingly common one among marketers in general. As commodity goods continue to proliferate, brand companies have sought new ways to differentiate themselves from their competitors. For example, Starbucks has made efforts to become an entertainment company, first selling CDs in its stores, then financing films like *Akeelah and the Bee.*[2] Burger King's then new mascots embodied a similar approach, differentiating the company not by the nature of its product but by the sensation around it. Creepy though the King and the

Subservient Chicken might be, they helped suggest that Burger King is an edgy, forward-looking adult brand, while McDonald's remains a kid-focused, mundane burger joint.

Of course, just because Burger King critiques advergames does not automatically distance its recent titles from the form at large. Who could deny the fact that the mere representation of Burger King mascots—not to mention the flotilla of BK food products the player serves in *Sneak King*—are advertisements in the ordinary sense? Yet these three games are also not *just* advergames either; that is, there's something that separates *Pocketbike Racer* from the ubiquitous branded web game.

One difference is the platform on which the games are played. In-game placements and advertisements have certainly graced the Xbox 360 (including Cadillac's Xbox Live delivery of a free content pack of vehicles into Microsoft's *Project Gotham Racing* in 2006), but the Burger King games are the first titles developed from the ground up for that platform as advertisement—and with the exception of a game development contest sponsored by Doritos in 2009–10, they remain the only such specimens.[3] This feat was made possible partly by the technical and commercial evolution of the videogame industry. Blitz Games was able to create, test, and release three games for both Xboxes in less than a year thanks to a proprietary cross-platform engine and tool kit the studio uses for all its titles. And Burger King was able to license the games thanks to high-level negotiations with Microsoft executives.

But more sophisticated technology and business acumen still fail to explain why an advertising game released on Xbox 360 would constitute a significantly different strategy for game-based advertising. As it happens, Xbox 360 players closely match the young adult demographic that Burger King hoped to lure with its irreverent King and Subservient Chicken characters, customers the restaurant franchise believes it can steal away from McDonald's. In marketing terms, these are the consumers whom television has lost, who have become cynical toward traditional advertising. They're also the consumers who might empathize most with Burger King's promise of an edgy alternative to the cloying pretense of Ronald McDonald.

When seen in this light, the content of the Burger King Xbox games becomes less important than the method of delivery. Burger King used these games as a lure to draw Xbox owners into its stores to buy a Value Meal. This and this alone was the games' primary goal.

Such a strategy itself is nothing new. It is, in essence, the same as the Happy Meal toy: lure kids (and thereby families) to take a meal at their franchise in a world where fast-food joints grace every corner. In the world of marketing, it's called a *promotion*.

Promotions offer an incentive to patronize a vendor, which may have little or nothing to do with the business's products and services. Sweepstakes and contests are a kind of promotion, as are giveaways like toys in kid's meals. In the case of the Burger King Xbox games, the downright cheap cost per game further accentuates the promotion's power: would-be burger lovers who already own an Xbox 360 proved more than willing to fork over $4 for a videogame when the going rate for commercial titles easily reaches fifteen times that price.[4] While the costs associated with these games have been kept closely guarded by the participants, Burger King reportedly sold over three million copies of the games by the end of the promotion, and so at least that many value meals.[5] Burger King likely recovered many times more the cost of the promotion before accounting for actual food sales—a rare state of affairs in traditional advertising indeed.

We use the term *advergames* to describe videogames whose primary purpose is to promote a company's brand, products, or services through gameplay. And by those standards, Burger King's Xbox games indeed might not be best characterized as advergames: they do promote the brand and the products, but not as their primary purpose. They hope first to drive sales of products through incentives.

I suggest the name *promogames* to videogames whose primary purpose is to promote the purchase of a product or service secondary or incidental to the game itself. The Burger King games do not tell gamers why they should buy those burgers over other burgers, or over fried chicken. Instead, they give gamers a reason to buy Burger King hamburgers. While advergames promote a company and its products, promogames offer an incentive to consume the company's goods independent of the game's representational properties. We can imagine a variety of possible promogames, some with stronger advertising aspects, like these Burger King Xbox games, and others with weaker advertising features. For example, consider a hypothetical special edition, level, or episode of a popular original title like *Halo* or *Half-Life* given away with a minimum purchase. Promogames seem to offer particular opportunity for companies who think their target markets intersect with particular segments of the videogame-playing market.

As much as Burger King's promogames might seem wholly original, titles that could easily qualify for the designation appeared a quarter century ago. Back in 1983 Mattel Electronics' M Network label created *Kool-Aid Man* for the Atari Video Computer System and the Intellivision. The game would later be available for traditional retail purchase, but originally would-be virtual thirst-relievers ("Oh yeah!") had to send in Kool-Aid UPC symbols along with a small handling fee to get the game. Johnson and Johnson commissioned a similar title the same year, *Tooth Protectors,* which was available only by mail order from the company. And also in 1983 Purina offered *Chase the Chuckwagon,* similarly available only by mail order in exchange for UPCs and a handling charge.

While some critics (including myself) have discussed these titles as early examples of advergames, the games also show a compelling prehistory for promogames.[6] Just as Burger King uses the young adult demographic of the Xbox as a lure for their desired market, so General Foods, Johnson and Johnson, and Purina used the younger demographic of the Atari VCS and Intellivision as a lure for theirs. Of these three early promogames, *Chase the Chuckwagon* most resembles Burger King's effort. At the time the game was released, a popular Purina dog food commercial showed a dog chasing a small chuckwagon (the brand's mascot) through a kitchen. Like *Sneak King, Chase the Chuckwagon* was conceived as an adaptation of the theme of the TV spot meant to appeal to players who would be familiar with its sponsor's icon.

Games like these show us that a single perspective on advertising games is not just an inadequate way to understand the intersection of these two worlds today, but that it wasn't even adequate thirty years ago. No matter one's opinion about the relative merits or dangers of advertisers' continued invasion of games, we must try to understand approaches to videogame-based advertising in complex ways—not just as developers or advertisers interested in creating new games but also as game players interested in understanding how and why brand companies seek to persuade us to consume their products.

10
Snapshots

In the late nineteenth century, photographs were primarily made on huge plate-film cameras with bellows and expensive hand-ground lenses. Their operation was nontrivial and required professional expertise. The relative youth of photography as a medium made that expertise much more scarce than it is today. All that changed when Kodak introduced the Brownie Camera in 1900.

The Brownie was different. It was about as simple as cameras get: a cardboard box with a fixed-focus lens and a film spool at the back. It took two-and-a-quarter-inch-square photos on 117 roll film, which George Eastman had first used a decade earlier. The simplicity of Brownie cameras made them reliable, and their low cost (around $25 in today's dollars when introduced in 1900) made them a low-risk purchase for families or even children. Millions were sold through the 1960s.

Both camera and film were cheap enough to make photography viable. Easy development without a darkroom made prints possible for everyone. The Brownie, and later the 35 mm camera that replaced it, didn't just simplify the process of making pictures; they also ushered in a new kind of picture: the snapshot. Snapshots value ease of capture and personal value of photographs over artistic or social value.

The Brownie brought photography to the people, but not without some help. The snapshot concept was borrowed from a hunting term for shooting from the hip, but Eastman contextualized the act for the masses. For its advertising, Kodak coined the "Kodak moment" and encouraged photographers to "celebrate

< 70 >

the moments of your life," as they still do today. Eastman's promise was "You press the button and we do the rest."

More than a century after Eastman's simple roll cameras, today's computer culture values a similar strain of creative populism. Websites and software provide tools that promise to "democratize" the creative process. Cheaper, more powerful hardware and inexpensive, easy-to-use software have made professional video editing and DVD production available to everyone. No-investment on-demand printing has made CD and T-shirt manufacturing a snap. Blogs and one-off book printing services have made written publication easy.

Following this trend, several companies have attempted to do for videogames what the Brownie did for photography. Big players like Microsoft (Popfly Game Creator) and Electronic Arts (Sims Carnival) have gotten into the game-maker game, as have start-ups like Metaplace, Gamebrix, WildPockets, PlayCrafter, and Mockingbird. While many of these products have since been shuttered or changed direction, each offers a slightly different perspective on simplifying game creation.[1] Sims Carnival offers three methods: a wizard, an image customizer, and a downloadable visual-scripting tool. PlayCrafter relies on physics, Gamebrix on behaviors, Mockingbird on goals. Popfly uses templates.

As platforms, each tool relies on the formal properties of different sorts of games. Some differences are obvious: Sims Carnival's Wizard and Swapper tools let people create games easily by changing variables and uploading new art, while PlayCrafter automates physical interactions. Formal distinctions are a common way to simplify the creation of games. Long before Sims Carnival and its brethren, desktop game-creation software used genre conventions as the formal model for add-assets-and-script type tools: *GameMaker* fashions tile-based action/arcade games; *Adventure Game Studio* makes graphical adventures; *RPGMaker* outputs role-playing games.[2]

A focus on formal constraints—character statistics or genre

distinctions like moving from screen to screen—makes sense from a tool developer's perspective: different sorts of games require different kinds of programmatic infrastructures. But from the lay creator's perspective, genre is a less useful starting point than topic. "I want to make a game about my cat" is a different sentiment than "I want to make a graphical adventure game." Photography doesn't make such a distinction; a camera can just as easily take a landscape as a portrait.

A fundamental difference between Eastman's Brownie and today's DIY game tools emerges: there's no videogame equivalent to the camera. Game creation can never become a fully automated affair. Taking a photograph is easy partly because so much of the process goes on without us. After you "press the button," to use Eastman's words, light bends through a lens onto the emulsion of a film or the light-sensitive surface of a charge-coupled device (CCD). Film development can be outsourced to Wal-Mart, and digital images are ready for immediate printing or posting. Video is similar; editing, titles, and sound are all optional but easily added with tools that come with every modern computer. Writing isn't as automated as image making, but it's a skill everyone uses in daily life. But printing or publishing are better facilitated by new digital tools.

Conversely, videogame creation exercises few common skills. It requires programming of some kind, or puppeteering a tool that does the programming behind the scenes. It requires animation, sound design, and environmental design. It requires designing for interaction, which can be complex even when the result is simple. It requires careful tuning even just to produce an experience that functions, let alone functions interestingly. There is simply no magic box we can put in front of the world that, when a button is pressed, turns what it sees into a videogame.

People were already fairly accustomed to using and creating images, video, and writing before the social web came along to make it easier to distribute them. That doesn't mean people were creating *good* images, video, and writing: just think of the last time you sat through someone's child's birthday party video, perused their family photo album, or read the sappy poetry from their courtship. The reason other people's cherished objects are just crap to you, to borrow a line from George Carlin, is because they've invested them with sentimental meaning. A snapshot has value only for the very few, even if it can be shown to the many.

This is a principle many celebrations of web 2.0 misunderstand. The long-tail economics of web aggregators make a business out of offering high-quality content for everyone, low-quality content for no one, and everything in-between. Despite the tabloidesque tales of ordinary people made YouTube stars that litter popular magazines, the fundamental benefit of simple creation and publishing tools lies in their ability to let people make things for one another on a very small scale, one traditional marketplaces can't sustain.

And what are the things people tend to make first, for the smallest audiences? Personal things, things that let them share experiences with their friends or family. Snapshots, of various sorts. All of those millions of photos or videos or blogs about vacations or pet tricks or hobbies add up. The outcome of such work isn't important because it's good; it's important because it holds meaning for creators and their kin. No matter what the venture capitalists and technology pundits may say about sharing and aggregation, YouTube and Flickr and the like function as social media because they function first as private media. Our notion of "private" has just expanded somewhat.

A close look at products like Sims Carnival reveals many snapshot games hidden among the much less interesting DIY attempts at mainstream casual games. Games about crushes, games celebrating birthdays, games poking fun at celebrities. That site even has an "e-card" section for such games, and premade templates to create games about kissing a date, icing a birthday cake, or celebrating the holidays. Sims Carnival's tools make the customization process more like Eastman's "we'll do the rest." It's easy for someone to insert fixed assets like text and images—the things they already learned how to create easily in previous eras. As a result, the most successful snapshots on Sims Carnival are not good games compared with casual games, and it's wrongheaded to compare the two. Rather, the successful snapshots are good games *for their creators* and those with whom they might share their efforts.

Consider a particularly telling example, *Dad's Coffee Shop*. The game was created with the Swapper tool, by replacing a few assets from the stock game *Fill the Order,* a simple cake shop game. The gameplay is identical; the player drags the correct cake to match a passing customer's request. *Dad's Coffee Shop*'s creator has added occasional photos of her parents, and this important description: "In loving and respectful memory of my father who never met a stranger." Like a snapshot, the game has value because of the way it lets its creator preserve and share a sentiment about her family. Likewise, you and I can appreciate it not as the crappy casual game that it is but as the touching personal snapshot that it is as well.

Or consider *You're Invited to go to heaven,* a simple quiz game created in Sims Carnival's Wizard tool, which asks a series of step-by-step questions to generate a game. *You're Invited* is a rudimentary example of Christian evangelism. The game poses just a single question, "Who is the Lord of your life?," and offers four answers: Chris Brown, Orlando Bloom, Zac Efron, and Jesus Christ. The "correct" choice is obvious, and it's tempting to write off this game as trite, even worthless. Its single question would seem barely to qualify it as a quiz game, a genre itself on the very fringes of the medium. But there's something deliberate and honest about its simplicity: this is not a game meant to inspire converts or even head-scratching; it's just a little touchstone in someone's day for reinforcing what's really important to the believer. The game somewhat resembles the inspirational photo or message pinned to a refrigerator or carried in a wallet. It serves a simple function: to remind its player that God is the only figure worthy of worship.

If *You're Invited to go to heaven* offers a modest critique of the sea of media fandom, plenty of other snapshot games on Sims Carnival do just the opposite, celebrating a favorite personality cult. At one point the service erupted with games featuring the teen idol Joe Jonas. One popular specimen is *Wash Joe Jonas,* a variation of a dog-washing original created by Sims Carnival staffers. As with most snapshot games, gameplay is quick and almost meaningless on its own: the player moves a mouse frantically to suds up Jonas before time runs out. Its purpose is simple and obvious: it offers a simulation of an intimate (if weird) relationship with a pop icon, one the player is unlikely ever to experience in real life. The game functions like a wall poster or a printed notebook, or even like a Photoshop job that inserts teen beside heartthrob. When played, the game works as a kind of snapshot effigy, a thing to create sighs and coos and then to be put down again.

"Democratization" is an awfully haughty way to describe new ways to use old media, but it's a term you often hear among Internet entrepreneurs and journalists. Eastman's cameras were "for the masses," like the Model T, and web services like YouTube and CafePress certainly are as well. But whether they deserve to be confused with self-governance and citizenship is another matter. Silicon Valley's libertarian tendencies conflate technological progress and social progress. Another conception is needed.

There are lots of things one can do with web-based game-making services. One of them is to try to create hit games that generate ad revenue and earn public renown. Another is to create artgames meant to characterize the human condition. But perhaps the most interesting uses of these tools are the ones that so closely resemble snapshots in spirit and function.

Some inventions, like the Brownie, make a previously complex creative process much easier. Yet the Brownie alone did not invent informal photography. It was just a tool. People had to be taught how to use it, which Kodak did through a lot of hand-holding, careful marketing, and patience. Such is the next challenge for the videogame snapshot. In this respect, the Sims team's effort to seed its site with examples for remix is an admirable start. But they're examples that aspire a little too much toward real casual games, a notion reinforced by the site's traditional genre categories (action, adventure, racing, shooter).

The Brownie teaches us that snapshots aren't just good pictures created easily thanks to simple tools. They're also good pictures—or games—created for *different* purposes. The future of videogame snapshots will require platform creators to show their potential users how to incorporate games into their individual lives. The results could prove important. The snapshot didn't just popularize photography as disposable, it also helped greater numbers of ordinary people appreciate photography as craft. A successful game creation platform is one that fulfills such a role.

11
Texture

I enjoy the ancient Chinese strategy game Go, although I'm hardly an expert. The open-source GnuGO AI built into the computer version of the game I play overpowers me much of the time.

After many years of having gone without, I received a Go board and set of stones as a holiday gift. Immediately I noticed the most important difference between playing on the computer and off it: touching the board and the stones. I had forgotten how tactile a game like Go is. The black and white often have a different texture from one another, depending on the type and quality of stones one uses. The feel and weight of them between the fingers somehow aids the pondering that comes with their placement.

Once the player chooses a move, placing the stone on a real board offers a far more tactile challenge than clicking an on-screen goban. The stones move, so disrupting the board is an easy feat that must be carefully avoided. Traditionally, Go players would hold a stone between the index and middle finger and strike their move, so as to create a sharp click against the wooden board.

Go is a cerebral, minimalist game that exudes purity and austerity. Computer versions of Go adapt these values unflappably. Although purists favor silence in selecting and holding a stone, for me Go is a game of rummaging for a stone in a smooth wooden bowl and stroking it in thought before placing it to mark territory. These features are not unique to Go, but they're distinctive. In chess the pieces rest on the board, or off, never to be touched save to punctuate decision. Although both games are cerebral, Go is far more sensual. Go reminds us that the physical world—games

< 77 >

included—have *texture*. They offer tactile sensations that people find interesting on their own.

In painting, texture is an acknowledged aspect of creativity. The word describes the weave of the canvas, the application of the medium on it, and the interaction of the two. It is a feature that frequently earns mention among critics and casual observers alike as a fundamental part of the finished work.

Postimpressionist painters like Vincent van Gogh used thick applications of paint, partly to re-create the effects of light on the surface of the canvas itself as well as in the subjects represented. And Jackson Pollock's abstract expressionist work relies almost entirely on texture; Pollock even added grains of sand and shards of glass to his already viscous industrial paints to increase the texture of the finished work.

Other media adopt their own understandings of texture. In the culinary arts, texture refers to the physical sensation of a food in one's mouth, such as the crispness of a cucumber or the slipperiness of an oyster. And in music, texture is used metaphorically to refer to the relationship between sounds and voices in a piece—as if they were layered through time like paint on a canvas.

In the computational arts, the term *texture* usually appears only in technical speak. Textures are the graphical skins laid atop 3-D models so they appear to have surface detail. Texturing techniques like bump mapping and normal mapping use 2-D image data to perturb the lighting patterns applied to objects by 3-D rendering algorithms to make them appear to have a surface texture not actually present in the 3-D model itself. These simulate the appearance, but not the behavior or sensation, of texture. This is nothing new; the fine arts have often done similar things. The artist Réne Magritte was particularly adept at creating the appearance of texture in his subjects with color and tone rather than paint thickness. In "Le modèle rouge," for example, the texture of the wood slats and the dirt ground jump out as familiar textures, despite the flatness of Magritte's brush technique.

But unlike paintings and plats principaux, games are not static scenes or objects—they're interactive models of experiences. To simulate the behavior, rather than just the appearance of texture, games have to use more than visual effects. Sound design is one answer: footfalls or bullet casings can produce different noises when falling on grass, dirt, concrete, wood. A character wading through tall grasses causes their blades to swoosh. When steered off the road, a car's tires grind against gravel.

Simulated properties of the physical world can also contribute to texture. A game might slow a character's movement through brush or swamp, as do both realistic first-person shooters like *Far Cry* and abstract strategy games like *Advance Wars.* Likewise, driving games from *Pole Position* to *Burnout: Paradise* alter a vehicle's speed and handling when it moves across different surfaces, simulating the differences in traction. Friction is another frequently simulated texture: platformer games like *Ice Climber* simulate the reduced friction of ice-covered surfaces.

In all these cases, videogames simulate the texture of the real world in two ways: through visual appearance or effects. A stone cavern wall or a splintered wood floor communicates texture by appearance. Contemporary graphics processing units make the surface textures of objects in games appear lifelike, just like the wood slats in Magritte's painting. When the player moves around in these worlds, the renderer's real-time updates reinforce the sense of texture in the scene by offering different views of the same surfaces.

The driver's shoulder and the soldier's swamp communicate texture by effect. When the player operates machines or moves creatures, their behaviors are constrained by the physical consequences certain textures represent. In such cases, the player still does not *feel* the texture of the road or the brush of the grasses during play, but only the cold plastic of the controller. Unlike painting and sculpture (which forbid touch) and music (which cannot accommodate it), videogames *require* user participation.

Even though image and sound make up much of their raw output, touch is an undeniable factor of gameplay.

Force feedback, motion simulation, and vibration have been built into expensive flight and military training simulators for decades. By the 1980s some of this technology made its way into the arcade. The 1988 coin-op sim *Hard Drivin'* featured force feedback steering, which resisted player rotation at higher speeds and rumbled on collision. Tactile computer interfaces (sometimes called *haptics*) had become a consumer industry by the early 1990s, with companies like Immersion developing cheaper, simpler sensors and motors that allowed such devices to be integrated into objects other than the expensive, awkward gloves and vests of dedicated virtual reality labs.

Thanks to the Nintendo 64 Rumble Pak add-on, we usually give the term *rumble* to haptic feedback in videogames. Rumble allows games to create tactile sensations in addition to visual and aural ones; for example, cars might seem to bump with the changing texture of asphalt, gravel, dirt. Technically, rumble in contemporary game systems is more or less the same: motors spin one or more unevenly molded weights in a housing within a controller's body. But despite the simplicity of rumble, its effects are quite varied: the pulse of a heartbeat signifies health and instills fear in *Silent Hill*; a tackle in *Madden NFL* registers physically as well as visually; the tremor of a gunshot in *Call of Duty* alerts the player to unseen dangers from behind or above; the vibration of the steering wheel in *Gran Turismo* communicates the force of cornering a hairpin at speed; the subtle signal of a motor signals the cursor entering a button in the *Wii Sports* menu screen; a jolt to the hand in *MVP Baseball* alerts the player to an opponent stealing a base; a spin of the rumble pak in *The Legend of Zelda: The Ocarina of Time* signifies the loose feel beneath Link's feet when a treasure is buried beneath the ground he stands on.

In general, the use of rumble is of two kinds: the first is increased immersion. Rumble is supposed to make the player feel more a part of the game in titles like *Madden* or *Silent Hill.* The second is *better feedback.* In *Wii Sports* and *The Legend of Zelda,* rumble helps the player orient toward interface or gameplay goals. But despite the utility of rumble in these cases, there's something missing. Rumble infrequently communicates texture in the way that paint, food, or even 3-D bump mapping does: the texture always has purpose, never just aesthetics. Put differently, rumble is an instrumental kind of texturing: it makes the environment tactile only to allow the user to make better progress within it. Even 3-D rendered texture is not so brazen about its focus on function: one can comfortably look in simple admiration at the walls and floorboards of a room in *Half-Life 2.*

There's at least one example of a game that uses rumble to provide direct, tactile *sensation* instead of feedback. And surprisingly, this title relies on a musical rather than physical texture as its primary tactile inspiration. Tetsuya Mizuguchi's *Rez* is a psychedelic, abstract rail shooter first released for Sega Dreamcast in 2001. The game is set in the data flow of a computer network, where the player takes on the role of a hacker trying to reboot the system while destroying enemies like viruses.

Mizuguchi cited synesthesia—sense impressions that relate to different senses than the ones that stimulate them—as an inspiration for the game. It combines striking visual, musical, and manipulative experiences all at once. As a part of this goal, the Japanese special edition of the PlayStation 2 version of the game included a "trance vibrator," a large plastic dongle that plugs into the console via USB. The device has no inputs, but houses a rumble motor within.

When *Rez* is played with the trance vibrator active, the device pulses in time with the trance electronica music that plays during the game. The music, in turn, signals the position of enemies in time with the beat. The player already has a tactile relationship with the music via timed button presses on the controller, but the trance vibrator offers an experience of the music's texture, translated into continuous tactile sensations, at the same time that the musical texture is also translated visually into neon abstractions.

Although Mizuguchi denies that the trance vibrator was intended to be a sexual add-on for *Rez,* that obvious use has been well documented.[1] The potential for sexual pleasure only underscores how *Rez*'s use of rumble focuses on a different kind of tactility than does *Halo* or *Gran Turismo*: in *Rez, the player touches the surface of the game itself.* The texture of neon light and synth phrases produce a surface one can literally feel.

The abstraction and immoderation of sensation in *Rez* offers an extreme example of videogame texture, one few games could or should replicate. But *Rez* sends a signal that other games might wish to tune in: just as the texture of a tufted wool rug can please the toes, or the texture of an unagi atop a nigiri can please the tongue, so similar tactility can please the gamer's body. These are pleasures far more subtle and confounding than the anonymous fun of solving a problem in a game.

It might be possible to simulate the tactile pleasures of Go in a videogame. Removing the snap-to-grid stone placement would be a start. A physics simulation could allow perturbation of the stones when they touch, just as so many games do with crates and with barrels. A videogame adaptation could depict the bowls of stones and use a fluid dynamics model to allow the player to stir it while he or she considered a move, or to spin it in a virtual hand.

Such simulation might successfully refer to the tactility of the original, but that appreciation would quickly become conceptual, lost in the limitations of mouse or analog stick compared with fingers. Still, the potential is great. Developers render the visual aspects of videogame worlds in excruciating detail: the marbled, diffracted surfaces of water, the filthy grit of alleyways, the splintered grain of bombed-out church rafters. They render the visual and aural aspects of these worlds in startling vividness and at great expense. But those worlds remain imprisoned behind the glass of our televisions and our monitors. *Rez* shows us that as far as texture is concerned, games can be as much like food as they are like film.

12 Kitsch

Thomas Kinkade paints cottages, gardens, chapels, lighthouses, and small-town street scenes. He paints such subjects by the dozens each year, but he sells thousands of them for at least a thousand dollars each, all "originals" manufactured using a complex print process that involves both machine automation and assembly line–like human craftsmanship. The result has made Kinkade the most collected painter in history.

Unlike most working painters, Kinkade's work doesn't go out to exhibition or collection, his most "important" works later being mass-produced on prints or mugs or datebooks for the general public. No, Kinkade's work is mass-market from the get-go. Every subject, every canvas becomes an immediate widget to be marketed in every channel. The artist himself put it this way in a *60 Minutes* interview: "There's been million-seller books and million-seller CDs. But there hasn't been, until now, million-seller art. We have found a way to bring to millions of people, an art that they can understand."[1] For Kinkade, "an art they can understand" means tropes of nostalgia and idealism. He paints perfect small-town Main Streets with friendly neighbors and milkmen. He paints patriotic portraits of flapping flags. He paints white Christmases with serenading carolers. He paints glowing gardens basked in filtered beams of sunlight.

There's a name for this sort of art, an art urging overt sentimentality, focused on the overt application of convention, without particular originality: we call it *kitsch*.

Kitsch has a complicated history. A century and a half ago, fine art became a personal plaything of the cultural elite at the same

< 83 >

time as the middle classes proliferated thanks to industrialism. Then much as now, once a lower class catches a glimpse of the group just above it, it tends to mimic those styles and tastes in an effort to climb the social ladder. In nineteenth-century Europe, one way such longing for status took form was to acquire consumer-grade copies of art created in the style of the fine arts of the cultural elite. Eventually a marketplace grew around art for the masses, just as one exists today for Kinkade's paintings and trinkets and calendars and textiles and the like.

Are there kitsch games? Such games would have to accomplish the operation of kitsch as much as its appearance.

To start, they might have to draw on borrowed conventions, repurposing them for popular appeal. Lots of games do this, and it might be tempting to point to the glut of selfsame casual puzzle games and social games as likely candidates. But those games don't adopt another necessary property of kitsch: trite sentimentalism. Nor do they exhibit the necessary level of quality. While nineteenth-century kitsch painting was sometimes accused of having been thrown together, modern kitsch can have quite high production values—Kinkade's paintings are technically competent examples of a particular style of realism.

Ferry Halim's online web games, published on his Orisinal.com site since 2001, are perfect candidates for videogame kitsch. They borrow conventions from casual games, using simple mouse movement and button pressing as their sole controls. Thematically, the Orisinal games depict idyllic scenes of natural beauty and wholesomeness, riddled with cute critters and schmaltzy musical scores. And from the perspective of production, Halim's games are well executed, with high-quality illustration-style graphics, smooth animation, and fitting sound effects.

Take the first game published on the site, *Apple Season.* In the game, a hundred shiny, red apples fall from the top of the screen, accelerating as they spin. The player moves a small basket side to side at screen bottom, attempting to catch the apples. The source of the apples isn't shown, allowing the player to fill in the details:

perhaps they're falling from an unseen, noble orchard tree, waiting to be reaped by ruddy-faced families. The score display at the bottom adds the final packet of saccharine sweetness: apples are not caught but "saved." The noble player basks in this virtuous, if corny, victory.

Or consider *It Takes Two,* a game about helping a dog and cat help one another. Adorable, illustrated animals (a Halim trademark) stand at opposite sides of a seesaw. When the player clicks, the animal at the top jumps down, vaulting the other up to the platform at the top. The player attempts to time these jumps such that each animal captures treats that pass across the middle of the screen.

It Takes Two capitalizes on the metaphoric sentimentalism of working together. The dog and cat, so often thought to be at odds, collaborate (thanks to the player's intervention) to meet both their needs. A new age piano loop cements the game's already glaring mawkishness: if only we could all get along like the adorable puppy and kitten.

Or take another Orisinal game, *Rainmaker.* Here the player pilots an adorable lad atop a cloud. When clicked, he strikes a mallet against the cloud, causing rain to pour down. Meanwhile, black birds fly from side to side. The player must time and orient the rain showers such that they wash the blackness of the birds into a bright white, crows becoming doves. Again, the game's sentimental message is clear: the innocence of youth, represented by the boy-cloud, can overcome the world's sorrows, represented by the black birds. Secondarily, the rain—often an omen of despondency—can also deliver joy. The game can be succinctly summarized with cliché: *every cloud has a silver lining.*

Both *Rainmaker* and *It Takes Two* include Halim's characteristic style of the nostalgic halcyon of lived environments. In *It Takes Two,* the background includes a blissful, clean city block, light spewing from behind a building, Kinkadesque. In *Rainmaker,* the cloud and birds fly above an idealized city at golden hour, its rooftops blurred in a rudimentary but effective simulation of the shallow depth of field one might see on a postcard photograph. Like Kinkade's art, the games of Orisinal depict idealized versions of locations and situations that probably never existed, but which the players can enjoy occupying as if they had.

Halim's games are an easy target; I'd call him the Thomas Kinkade of videogames. But other sorts of games offer a quite different version of kitsch.

Diner Dash and its derivatives offer instructive examples of a kind of videogame kitsch that doesn't deploy naturalistic sentimentalism of the Kinkade variety, but occupational sentimentalism instead. In *Diner Dash,* the player starts as Flo, at the dawn of her career as a restaurateur. She begins in a simple, shabby diner—all that she can afford—and the player's job is to help her build a thriving restaurant.

As in the other "click-management" games the title inspired (so named because the player clicks on objects in the scene to manage a character's actions), play is accomplished through a simplification of move-and-collide convention: one clicks on tasks (patrons to seat, food to serve, dishes to clear), and Flo automatically attends to these tasks. Mastery is thus matter of successfully splitting attention between the tasks of increasing number and frequency. The idea of complex, multiaction challenge endemic to games is reduced to clicking the right object at the right time. It is here that we see the copying and dilution of convention typical of kitsch.

In *Diner Dash,* sentimentalism is accomplished by invoking the moral fortitude of hard work. It's a game in which a good work ethic, careful attention, and persistence always yield success. All of the other factors that make the work of a restaurateur such a thankless, risky proposition are abstracted. The random chance of location, the accident of patron tastes, the spleen of newspaper critics—none of these play a role in the world of *Diner Dash.*

If Ferry Halim is the Thomas Kinkade of videogames, *Diner Dash* is its motivational poster, espousing the application of Care, Resolve, Persistence, Attention and other ideals of the Protestant work ethic. Indeed, *Diner Dash*'s values are the very same ones that a viewer might imagine take place inside the shops and kitchens of Kinkade's charming towns and cottages. When one plays such games, persistence leads to success, and success leads to resources, which increase both influence and leverage. In *Diner Dash,* it's a bigger restaurant and more customers. In *Airport Mania,* a game in the same genre, it's a larger airport with more planes and passengers.

The idea is one that appeals strongly to people. Despite received ideals of Puritanism and the American Dream, modern life is riddled with a strong dose of unfairness and random circumstance. By surrounding oneself with posters, or games, that espouse ideals of control, the timeworn hope of pure will breeds the wistfulness that makes kitsch appealing.

Kitsch is often derided in the "real" art world for offering manufactured copies of ideas served to a dispassionate and accepting audience of consumers. This sentiment of rejection has remained more or less the same since the critics Max Horkheimer and Theodor Adorno first coined the term "culture industry" some sixty years ago.[2] Defenders argue that so-called manufactured culture is popular not because it manipulates people into falling back on hackneyed platitudes but because people like it in earnest. In truth, the truth of the matter matters little: whether or not making kitsch is a virtue or a vice is a question without answer. But for those who would seek such a purpose in games, one issue remains: kitsch was always meant to be *displayed,* to serve as a marker of an upward-looking bourgeoisie. It offers tactile evidence of sentimentality, and in doing so provides social purpose. Videogames cannot easily be hung in a foyer or displayed on a console table.

Perhaps the solution is not to make games more easily displayed but to anticipate the ways we display them. Facebook is one candidate. The news feed posts in which games like *FarmVille, FrontierVille, Pet Society,* and *City of Wonder* report player actions often resemble a shelf of knick-knacks. These games follow the kitsch tradition of adorable sentimentalism, too. After click-ing incessantly to help a cute bear fashion the trappings of a mock medieval festival, the player of *Ravenwood Fair* can post news feed stories about new visitors to his or her fair: a cute mouse image is saved to the player's Facebook profile along with the kitschy text, "New Visitor! My Fair is growing larger and I've gotten a New Visitor! Here are some coins for you so your fair can get a new visi-tor too!" Every few minutes, *Ravenwood Fair* offers rewards the player can give to a friend, trinkets like a bundle of balloons or a tombstone or a cluster of daisies.

The real purpose of such posts and gifts is the "viral spread" by which these games acquire new users. But the result also offers the closest analogue to kitschy home-display videogames have yet mustered. Instead of displaying the games themselves, players of Facebook games display the exhaust of gameplay, the kitschy vir-tual trinkets they amass in the process. This array of virtual trin-ketry might help realize the videogame equivalent of Kinkade's million-seller art. After all, Facebook games like *FarmVille* boast tens of millions of players, all clicking cows and crops to show their friends, just like they might display Kinkade cottage paint-ings or Precious Moments angel figurines.

13

Relaxation

There is an aphorism commonly invoked when comparing video-games with other media. Videogames, people say, are a "lean forward" medium, while others are "lean back" media. Leaning forward is associated with control, activity, and engagement. Leaning forward requires continuous attention, thought, and movement, even if it's just the movement of fingers on analog sticks and digital buttons. It's one of the features that distinguish games from television, even if the former are often played on the latter. Leaning back is associated with relaxation, passivity, and even gluttony—just think of all those snacks we eat slouched on the sofa in front of the television. Physical interfaces like the Wii remote or the *Dance Dance Revolution* dance pad raise the stakes further, asking the player to get up off the couch entirely.

Leaning forward is useful when the desired effect of a game is high attention and twitchiness. But what if we wanted another kind of experience from a game, from time to time at least: a relaxing lean-back experience—a Zen game.

Of the few attempts to create relaxation in games, *Journey to Wild Divine* is the most deliberate. It's marketed as a new age game, a game for wellness. Using a fingertip controller that measures heart rate and skin galvanic response, the player exerts control by attempting to manage this biofeedback. The player might have to regulate heart rate to balance a ball or aim a bow. *Wild Divine* assumes that relaxation is a medical matter, something in the body that can be measured by devices and reported as inter-action feedback.

< 89 >

It's an interesting technique, and it really works—at times, anyway. The game's physiological inputs are responsive, and reducing one's heart rate through slow breathing can indeed help accomplish tasks in the game. Yet, once completed, that sensation of calm often disappears. When the player succeeds at a task in *Wild Divine,* the game rewards that success with sudden bursts of vision and sound. As the film scholar Irene Chien has observed, these transitions can be so visually and aurally sensuous compared with the states that bring them about that they often upend the player's physical victory.[1]

Another example is the award-winning University of Southern California game *Cloud.* Its student creators claim *Cloud* offers "a relaxing, non-stressful, meditative experience."[2] To play, you manipulate a blue-haired character who flies to create clouds.

Cloud is a beautiful and unusual game, and both its fiction and aesthetics imply relaxation. But in practice, the game instills exactly the opposite sensation for me. The indirect control of *Wild Divine* attempts to alleviate the usual physical stressors of games. *Cloud* uses the mouse, but increases rather than reduces the precision required to use it. The player must grip the mouse tightly to accomplish the small variations in motion the game demands, struggling to get the character to move. Its controls frustrate more than they pacify.

The students who made *Cloud* incorporated under the shingle That Game Company, and they followed it up with the commercial title *flOw,* a game about growing a small underwater organism by eating floating detritus and parts of other creatures. *flOw* is simple but visually sensuous, taking advantage of the advanced graphics capabilities of the PlayStation 3, for which it was specifically developed. But as much as *flOw*'s spirit embraces relaxation, its sensations and themes also defy it.

Unlike games like *Rez* and *Geometry Wars,* which couple simple graphics to the pulsing beats of club electronica, *flOw* sets its glowing, procedural line art in the viscous silt of an unexplained underwater realm. Although it rejects the vivid chaos of electronica, *flOw* hardly takes on the hypnotic trance of house music let alone the waiting-room numb of soft jazz. Aurally, *flOw* lulls the player, but it blends that mollification with a barrage of seductive visuals. The result is a contradictory synesthesia, soothing gurgles of water combined with anxious bursts of light. *flOw*'s controls further emphasize this discomfort. Movement is accomplished solely via the PlayStation 3 controller's tilt sensors. Again the player must grasp and twist uncomfortably, using small movements that strain rather than calm. The white palms and throbbing head that punctuate a session of *flOw* are more reminiscent of drug abuse than meditation.

Moreover, *flOw* is a somewhat disturbing game. Borrowing from the psychological concept the game uses for its title, it offers the player control over rise and descent in the murk.[3] The creators suggest that this control allows the player to adjust the game's difficulty at will, designing a personalized path between challenge and boredom. But traversing each level requires devouring debris and other creatures to grow one's own character to the point that it can consume still larger ones on deeper levels. Simple though the creatures may be, the experience of attacking their central nodes to break them up and devour the remains is hardly a peaceful act. Though the game enforces no particular goals, the only viable option save abstinence is engorgement. Like the strip miner, the *flOw* player overwhelms everything in his or her path.

There are precedents for games that don't require the attention of a race car driver or the hallucination of a raver. The very term *casual game* already suggests leaning back, a more moderate commitment to playing. Yet not all casual games induce calm. For example, *Tetris* offers an example of a fast-paced abstract puzzle game where careful timing and split-second decisions influence success or failure. Such is the case for nondigital games like the word game Boggle or the stacking game Jenga, both of which come in multiplayer digital game versions.

But *Solitaire*, still the world's most widely distributed video-game thanks to being bundled with Microsoft Windows, makes no demands on time or attention. Like its tabletop counterpart, *Solitaire* waits patiently for the player to draw and place the next card. The digital version also takes all the annoying effort out of setting up a game. Clearing off the table and shuffling the deck are not required. Moved cards snap neatly onto piles. The player doesn't even have to enforce the rules, since the software does so automatically. Thus emerges the familiar image of the office worker, slumped in a chair, face on one hand, mouse in the other. *Solitaire*'s status as a feature of Windows makes it a perfect break from the demands of the workday. Sit back, zone out, move cards.

As casual games have evolved, variations on *Tetris* have been more popular than variations on *Solitaire*. Usually these come in the form of time constraints, whether by explicit clock, as in *Bejeweled*, or by mounting pressure, as in *Zuma*. As casual games publishers have come to realize that many players use these games for zoning out, they've partly adjusted their design and marketing strategies. PopCap now provides a stress-free version of *Bejeweled* and a version of *Chuzzle* with Zen mode, offering "a great on-the-go source of relaxation."[4]

Casual games inch closer to Zen because they're abstract. These games ask the player to move cards or blocks or stones into patterns. Unlike *Cloud* and *flOw*, the relationship between the objects and the patterns are arbitrary. The outcomes—clearing matches in *Bejeweled* or completing suit runs in *Solitaire*—matter less than the acts that create them. These games invite and measure repetitive gestures. They're akin to doodling on a napkin, or skimming through a magazine, or knitting in front of the television. Knitting, after all, is as much about keeping your hands busy in a predictable, ordered way as it is about making a sweater.

Will Wright has compared playing *SimCity* to gardening, suggesting that the methodical pruning of the city recalls the care of agronomy even more than that of urban planning.[5] Wright's use of gardening is metaphoric, but there are also more literal examples of videogame gardens that induce calm.

The *karesansui,* or Japanese dry garden, is a pit with rocks and sand that can be raked in the patterns of water ripples. Like meditation, the garden offers the visitor calm, presenting only a few objects of interest. It is often called a *Zen garden* in the West, a term that some Japanese garden proponents oppose for reasons of imprecision. No matter, the idea of tending to nature as a way to focus on oneself to elicit calm can be true of all kinds of gardening, from dry gardens to herb gardens.

Not all videogame gardens are Zen gardens though. *Viva Piñata* and *Pikmin* may take place in gardens, requiring tilling and planting and other horticultural pursuits, but they also demand considerable forward-leaning attention to ensure that a piñata evades attack, or a pikmin finds his way to work.

Other titles include more Zenlike gardening mechanics, even though they don't bill themselves as relaxation games. One is *Animal Crossing,* with its flower planting and tree axing. The most Zen of gardening activities in the game is also the most reviled. If you fail to visit your town for several days, weeds and clover start growing on the grass and pathways. If weeks or months go by, the weeds take over. Frustrating though it may seem at first, the process of systematically weeding an *Animal Crossing* town can be remarkably relaxing. Move, press B to weed, repeat. Sometimes you have to do it daily for weeks to fully overcome the undergrowth.

But the most Zen gardening in a videogame by far is in *Harvest Moon.* The daily reaping, milking, chicken lifting, and related chores require precision, duty, and calm. Crop watering is my pick for the most calming act, especially on the Gameboy or DS where the tile-based graphics more explicitly frame which square is which. *Harvest Moon* emphasizes the repetition of simple tasks as much as, if not more than, their outcomes. *Animal Crossing* and *Harvest Moon* are games that invite the player to complete these tasks independent of the long-term goals they facilitate. Both are games one might boot up late at night, before bed, to wind down. And unlike online social versions of farming like *FarmVille,*

Harvest Moon makes no social demands, no obligations to meet, no performances to better or virtual accomplishments to show off.

One finds fewer connections between walking and meditation, although new age relaxation remedies try to combine the two. No matter, the practice of meandering has been connected with salutary effects for centuries. Medieval labyrinths were thought to provide pathways to commune with God, a kind of surrogate pilgrimage. Henry David Thoreau wanders the ponds of Walden in the mid-nineteenth century at the same time as Charles Baudelaire wanders the streets of Paris, ennobling an increasingly alien environment with a kind of haphazard strolling, or *flânerie*.

The early PDP text adventure game *Colossal Cave* was inspired by Will Crowther's hobby of caving. Later adventure games like *Zork* and *The Legend of Zelda* continued the lineage of exploration as a part of the experience, but the persistence of riddles, puzzles, and enemies quickly make calm meandering in these games difficult. As so-called open world videogames have become more popular, so larger and more complex simulated environments are available for meandering. *Grand Theft Auto* and games of its ilk retain some of the nuisances of gameplay—police, rival gangs, and so forth—but their larger spaces also allow the player to hide from the game. One example is Jim Munroe's *My Trip to Liberty City*, a machinima (a movie produced inside a game) travelogue of Munroe's "walking tour" of *GTA III*'s urban landscape.

But the most meander-inducing of videogame saunters must be Yu Suzuki's *Shenmue*. Although it's an adventure game by genre, a combination of abstruseness and free movement in the game's Yokosuka district makes wandering around this quiet city its own reward. Passing time and changing weather in *Shenmue* vary this environment, as do similar dynamics in *Grand Theft Auto* and *Animal Crossing*. In a game like *Ico*, not knowing whether or not a door is usable can lead to frustration. But in *Shenmue*, the slow plod up stairs to a row of apartments offers strange satisfaction.

Because relaxation and meditation rely on inaction rather than action, they threaten to undermine the very nature of videogames. There's a fine line between producing Zen and satirizing it. The infamous, unreleased *Penn & Teller's Smoke and Mirrors* for Sega CD featured a minigame called Desert Bus, in which the player would make the eight-hour drive from Tucson to Las Vegas *in real time*, taking the wheel of a bus whose steering pulled slightly. Highway driving can indeed be calming, but Desert Bus is probably more conceptual art than meditation game.[6]

As *Animal Crossing* invites, a real meditation game would reject graphical sensuality in favor of simplicity and austerity. I have had my own go at one, called *Guru Meditation,* a meditation game for the Atari Video Computer System, which is played using an arcane 1982 Amiga peripheral called the Joyboard. In addition to its primary role as relaxation, the game also pays homage to an apocryphal story about how Amiga engineers tried to sit still on the Joyboard's plastic platform to recover from frustrating kernel panics during the authoring of the Amiga OS. My version is designed to be played by sitting cross-legged on the Joyboard, without moving. Responding to *flOw* and *Wild Divine*'s unfortunate conflation of tranquillity and visual sensuousness, *Guru Meditation* takes advantage of the Atari's more primitive graphics to de-emphasize a sensation of the outside world, in favor of an inner one.

To consider meditation games for platforms more commercially viable than the Atari VCS, one thing becomes clear: as designers and players, we must reject the principle of engagement. Relaxation and reflection arise from constrained environments in which the senses are de-emphasized and focused rather than escalated and expanded. Videogames may often overwhelm and titillate our senses, but relaxation comes instead from withdrawal and placidity. To relax through a game requires abandoning the value of leaning forward and focusing on how games can also allow players to achieve satisfaction by leaning back.

14 Throwaways

Casual games have become an increasingly more popular and important part of the videogame landscape. Proponents argue that casual games both open up new audiences for games and make new styles of games possible, but the genre has largely floundered in a swamp of copycat titles. One reason for this is a lack of imagination about what *casual* might mean. Here's an alternative: casual games are games that players use and toss aside, one-play stands, serendipitous encounters never to be seen again.

According to the International Game Developers Association (IGDA), casual games "generally involve less complicated game controls and overall complexity in terms of gameplay or investment required to get through game[s]."[1] The group contrasts casual games with "hardcore" or "core" or "traditional" games—games "developed for and delivered on a dedicated game console" that "involve more complicated game controls and overall complexity in terms of gameplay or investment required to get through game[s]." The IGDA white paper's authors admit "the typical casual gamer is hard to define," but suggest that the name characterizes "gamers who play games for enjoyment and relaxation." Casual games are less complex than core games and require lower commitment to both title and medium.

We might summarize the industry's conception of casual games along two axes: design considerations and player resources. Because casual gamers don't play many games or don't play them very often, they're unfamiliar with the complex conventions that might be second nature to hardcore gamers. These games attempt to minimize complexity and investment in player time,

< 96 >

money, and control mastery. Casual games sport designs and controls of reduced complexity that take little time to learn and to play, that come at modest cost and are easy to purchase. Such titles offer short gameplay sessions, measured in minutes rather than hours. They are marketed modestly, to be sold from websites or app stores for play on personal computers and mobile phones.

The typical design values of casual games strongly resemble the early coin-op industry. Consider controls. In 1971 Nolan Bushnell and Ted Dabny created *Computer Space,* a port of the popular minicomputer game *Space War!,* which the public would never have encountered outside research labs. It didn't sell well, a failing Bushnell has always pinned on complexity. As Bushnell explains, "You had to read the instructions before you could play, people didn't want to read instructions."[2] *Pong* fixed the problem. "To be successful," says Bushnell, "I had to come up with a game people already knew how to play; something so simple that any drunk in any bar could play." The *Pong* cabinet features one instruction: "Avoid missing ball for high score."

One can easily draw a connection between the tavern-going *Pong* player and the after-bedtime *Bejeweled* player. Indeed, the IGDA's casual games special interest group explicitly recommends mouse-only control for casual games ("The interaction between the user and the game should be limited to the computer mouse"). A mouse is something every computer user owns and knows how to use. Simple controls on existing equipment seem to be well-addressed design strategies in casual games.

As for money, the business model for coin-op games is somewhat different from that of desktop or web-based casual games. When designing games for the bar or arcade, developers aimed for short sessions, usually around two to three minutes. Such tactics maximized "coin drop," the cash the game could acquire in a fixed amount of time. Coin-op publishers looked to sell a large number of lower-priced plays of the same game, and to rely on repeat purchases of that game. This dynamic naturally encouraged a particular kind of competitiveness: players who get better at the game can play longer for less money, effectively reducing the publisher's incremental profit while maximizing the value of player's own leisure dollar.

In their heyday, coin-op games were easy to access—they were found in bars and convenience stores and Laundromats, places one would go regularly for reasons other than videogame play. Coin-op games were also low cost, usually just a single coin. By contrast, most casual games are accessed on or purchased from online portals. Players download, try, and then purchase, usually for $20 or so. There's no doubt that online purchasing offers easy access, one of the industry's design values. But is $20 really low cost? It's one-half to one-third the price of contemporary console games but still a considerable figure for a discretionary purchase. It's more than ten times as much as the average price of mobile games, for example, those available in Apple's App Store for iPhone and iPad.[3]

But the most contradictory of these three player resources is time. A common design philosophy for casual games is "easy to learn, hard to master" (for more on this, see chapter 18, "Habituation"). Casual games are supposed to respect the value of their players' time, making it easier to learn to play the game. But the notion of mastery raises doubt about low commitment in casual games. Individual casual game sessions often do require only short amounts of time: a round of *Solitaire* or *Tetris* or *Bejeweled* might take less than five minutes. But the maxim "easy to learn, hard to master" reveals that casual games actually demand significant *total* playtime. Players are expected to string short sessions together, either at once or over long periods, to maximize performance.

A casual games proponent might argue that the player might choose *not* to master the game but just to play short sessions early in the title's progression ("games you can play for five minutes or five hours"). But the business of casual games belies such an argument: for one part, the typical cost of a downloadable game suggests that medium- to long-term player commitment is required to get value from a purchase; for another part, downloadable games' 1–2 percent conversion on try-before-you-buy purchases suggests that the vast majority of players are satisfied with the gameplay experience of the trial anyway. Mastery demands high, not low commitment.

High commitment and long total time investment seem to contradict the very idea of casual games. The IGDA whitepaper authors even admit that "casual" is a somewhat inappropriate appellation: "Without a doubt, the term 'casual games' is sometimes an awkward and ill-fitting term . . . the term 'casual' doesn't accurately depict that these games can be quite addictive, often delivering hours of entertainment similar to that provided by more traditional console games." What, then, is the true meaning of *casual* in casual games?

The genre's current conception of "casualness" suggests informality rather than simplicity. If core or hardcore games are "formal" in the sense that they require adherence to complex gameplay and social conventions, then casual games are "informal" in the sense that they don't require such strict adherence. Informality is a kind of dressing-down of an otherwise more proper gaming practice. But informality also underscores the likelihood of regular, repetitive engagement with that practice. This is the *casual* of casual dress or casual Friday, both of which articulate a respite from the formality of business or social attire and mannerisms. Casual Friday is a repetitive, habitual casualness: come as you are, but expect to do it every week.

Applied to games, casual as informality characterizes the notions of pickup play common in casual games while still calling for repetition and mastery. This is why casual games can value both short-session duration and high replayability or addictiveness. Casual games may allow short sessions, but they demand high total playtime, and therefore high total time commitment on the player's part. Low commitment represents the primary unexplored design space in the casual games market.

To understand what other design opportunities might exist for casual games, or what other kinds of games this sector of the industry may have ignored, it's worth asking what other meanings the term *casual* possesses in ordinary parlance, outside the domain of videogames. Here are a few:

Casual as Indifferent—we sometimes use *casual* to refer to a lack of concern, or even a feeling of indifference. In this sense, *casual* conjures notions of apathy, insouciance, and nonchalance.

Casual as Spontaneous—we also use *casual* to refer to spontaneity or offhandedness. In this sense, *casual* raises notions of unpremeditated action, doing something off-the-cuff.

Casual as Fleeting—and we also sometimes use *casual* to refer to something short-lived and momentary, something superficial, like a temporary or part-time commitment, or an irregular activity.

These senses of casual all contain properties of freedom, superficiality, and even flippancy. Such properties correspond well with the notion of low commitment left unexplored in casual games. If casual Friday is the metaphor that drives casual games as we know them now, then casual sex might offer a metaphor to summarize the field's unexplored territory. If casual games (as in Friday) focus on simplicity and short individual play sessions that contribute to long-term mastery and repetition, then casual games (as in sex) focus on simplicity and short play that might not ever be repeated—or even remembered.

Editorial "newsgames" offer one possible example of such games. These are videogames created in response to specific, real-world events that recount or comment on them; Gonzalo Frasca has called them the videogame equivalent of editorial cartoons.[4] Frasca launched the concept on Newsgaming.com with an example, *September 12th: A Toy World,* a commentary about Western retaliation, in particular the U.S. response to September 11, 2001.

September 12th was not necessarily intended to be played over and over again. The game's mechanics reveal its commentary through revelation rather than mastery. Still, *September 12th* is not as fleeting as it might be; it's loosely coupled to the events it comments on. The game was released in October 2003, so timeliness wasn't its guiding design principle, and admittedly the game attracted more attention and response as a political game than as a newsgame. The game refers to an entire era of U.S. foreign policy. Other newsgames use the genre's coupling to current events to create more specific, more disposable experiences.

Consider *Zidane Head-Butt*, a very simple game created and released less than a day after Zinedine Zidane's infamous and shameful head-butt of Marco Materazzi during the 2006 World Cup final. The game is crude at best, its gameplay little more than a modification of whack-a-mole, as the player controls Zidane and clicks the mouse to head-butt an endless barrage of Materazzis. The game's sole, simple mechanic offers no novel experience. It's yet another skinned whack-a-mole. The game even lacks a score tally. As such, *Zidane Head-Butt* stands mostly as a curiosity, a media gimmick released quickly enough to capitalize on the hubbub surrounding the event itself.

But rather than reject the game's significance based on its crude implementation or simplistic conception, we should celebrate *Zidane Head-Butt* precisely for its fleeting nature. This is not a game one attempts to master—indeed it's probably not even a game one plays a second time. By maximizing curiosity, the game successfully adheres to the casual game design value of very low time commitment. This is a game one plays once, then forgets about forever—but that one forgets without gaining much meaningful insight about the event it re-creates.

September 12th is too loosely coupled to the events it editorializes to become fleeting in the way a casual (as in sex) game might do, but it offers meaningful commentary on the events in question. Conversely, *Zidane Head-Butt* is too trivial to offer any commentary whatsoever (it's really a tabloid game, not an editorial game), but it's highly disposable. Other newsgames have attempted to combine these two virtues.

The Arcade Wire: Airport Security might be such a one, created by my studio Persuasive Games shortly after the fall 2006 ban on liquids in carry-ons. The gameplay is simple, like the other examples discussed above: the player takes the role of a U.S. Transportation Security Administration (TSA) agent, who must work under satirically overstated conditions of constantly changing security rules. The player might be asked to remove every passenger's pants, or to confiscate hummus or pressurized cheese.

With *Airport Security*, we tried to strike a convincing balance between political commentary and promiscuous play. When newspaper readers take in a traditional editorial cartoon, they may linger on it for a few minutes, enjoying its satire or disputing its biting commentary. But soon enough, they turn the page, the cartoon left to be forgotten forever. This type of casual experience corresponds much more strongly with low-complexity time commitment first proposed above: the player not only plays the game for only a few minutes (the game seems designed coin-op style, to enforce a loss in three minutes' time or less) but also leaves the play experience having consumed a legitimate commentary on the relationship between arbitrary rule changes and airport security.

Newsgames in general offer a promising example of the expanded uses of videogames, an application I have discussed extensively in a book I coauthored on the subject (*Newsgames: Journalism at Play*).[5] But newsgames offer an insight into the expanded *experience* of videogames as much as their expanded *function*. In that respect, current event newsgames are just one example of casual games (as in sex); surely there are more games that might rescue the very genre from its noisy doldrums. Most game developers are "core gamers," well versed in the complex logics of resource allocation. They tend to privilege simplicity and emergence in games, favoring sophisticated experiences that create new challenges each time we play. And perhaps one well-balanced, mastery-style casual game is less financially risky than many throwaway experiences. But such an attitude ignores the pleasures of the fleeting, the transitory, the impermanent. Casual games, perhaps, can do more by hardly doing anything at all.

15
Titillation

Soon after the release of *Grand Theft Auto: San Andreas* in 2005, the Dutch hacker Patrick Wildenborg uncovered a hidden sex scene in it.[1] The scene in question was never intended to appear in the game, but its assets had been left on the disk, presumably owing to a cut late in the development process. Two years later, a furor erupted over a sex scene in the sci-fi role-playing game *Mass Effect*. The scene even had the potential to involve alien lesbianism for some players, depending on the relationships a player had built up in the many hours preceding it.[2] For the same reason, other players might not have encountered it at all. Even though both were far less explicit than sex scenes in R-rated movies or on cable television, enormous controversy erupted around them.[3]

These examples underscore just how scarce and touchy sex in games still is. Fear of sex in the ratings process and the marketplace makes legitimate eroticism difficult in traditional commercial games—the depiction of anything more than toplessness all but guarantees that a game won't receive the R-equivalent MA rating in the United States, dooming it to retail obscurity. But the lack of a viable "unrated" commercial games market—whether for explicit sex or other types of content—makes it easy to forget that there was once a place for sexually off-color games.[4]

Leisure Suit Larry, Al Lowe's 1987 series of adult adventure games, offers one precedent, but there was another game five years before that, on the Atari Video Computer System. The primary adult game developer for Atari was Mystique, a spinoff of an American film pornographer. Mystique released several porn games for the system in 1982. They were all labeled as "Swedish

< 103 >

Erotica," but this was just marketing—they were homegrown in the USA. The games were sold as adult entertainment, not as games, and would have been available only at adult specialty shops, video stores, and the like. Each box sported an all-caps warning: "NOT FOR SALE TO MINORS."

The best-known title is certainly *Custer's Revenge,* because it was also the most offensive. In the game, the player pilots a naked Custer character with cowboy hat and enormous, erect penis across a field of flying arrows in order to rape a Native American woman tied to a post. Not much more needs to be said about this one.

Another Mystique title was *Beat 'Em & Eat 'Em,* a clone of Larry Kaplan and David Crane's popular 1981 game *Kaboom!* The player controls a pair of naked women who move along a street. The computer controls a naked man on top of a building, who ejaculates copiously from the roof. The player must steer the women to catch the falling ejaculate in their open, upturned mouths. "Should you miss," explains the game manual, "shame on you. After all, it could have been a famous doctor or lawyer." The game also awards an extra life every time the score reaches sixty-nine.

Despite the primitive nature of the Atari VCS compared with modern game consoles, the creators of *Beat 'Em & Eat 'Em* knew that they'd have to pay close attention to the appearance of its actors—their brand of pornography is visual, after all. The Atari VCS is capable of displaying two sprites at a time—that is, its graphics hardware allows the programmer to store two one-byte sprite values at once. More sprites can appear to be on the screen by reusing these registers at different vertical locations on the screen. In *Beat 'Em & Eat 'Em,* the women are doubled by flipping a bit on another register to stretch or multiply the sprites, so they appear as a pair. But there's no concept of color-bitmapped graphics on the VCS. Instead, colors for each of the two sprites must be set manually. Because of timing constraints, color changes typically happen on a line-by-line, not a pixel-by-pixel, basis.

A close inspection of the screen reveals that the women have carefully detailed nipples and pubic hair, as well as blonde locks that wrap around their faces. This is not something the Atari can do without some coaxing. The body is one sprite, running the whole length of the character without color changes. The hair is the second sprite, horizontally positioned atop the first. To render the nipples, the second sprite is also used, but its color is changed in the lines after the end of the hair. Then it's changed back to yellow on the following scan line. I draw attention to these details because they demonstrate just how much effort had to be put into renditions of the naked female form. The Mystique games have been accused of being low-quality titles with poor production values. But details like this suggest the opposite; a lot of love went into these games—a certain kind of love, anyway.

Despite such creativity, after the crash of 1983 Mystique went out of business, along with most other independent developers. The rights to their games were transferred to Playaround, which rereleased these games and a few more on "double-ender" cartridges (two games attached back-to-back—I'm sure I don't need to belabor the double entendre). Playaround added new versions of the Mystique games that swap the roles. These include *Bachelorette Party,* which swapped the gender roles of Mystique's *Breakout* clone *Bachelor Party,* and then a version of *Beat 'Em & Eat 'Em* called *Philly Flasher,* in which the roles are also reversed. Playaround also produced new versions of *Custer's Revenge* for the European market, again one with each role, called *General Retreat* and *Westward Ho.* These were never sold stateside because of the controversy over *Custer's Revenge.*

Playaround also created original adult games, each offering play as both the male and female role. One was *Knight on the Town/Lady in Wading,* in which a knight/Amazon must build a bridge across a moat to rescue a princess/prince. Another was *Burning Desire/Jungle Fever,* in which a naked man/woman flying a helicopter must ejaculate/lactate out a fire that risks devouring a man/woman tied to a stake. And in *Cathouse Blues/Gigolo* the player helps a man/woman score with seven partners in a neighborhood while avoiding alarm-rigged houses and police.

Despite their relatively sophisticated computer renditions of nudity (given the era and the platform constraints, anyway), the Mystique/Playaround games don't engage adult sexual fantasies very effectively. They sometimes amuse, but they mostly offend. Arousal is relative to some extent, but the games don't live up to the truly adult expectations Mystique sets in the manuals—it's hard to imagine anyone using them earnestly as pornography. Some of these expectations are clearly written in jest, like this one about how to start the game:

> With the power shut off, gently insert your Mystique video game cartridge into your Atari VCS Video Computer System in the same manner as you would with any compatible game cartridge. Turning the switch "on" will activate the "foreplay" mode. This is very similar to the "attract" mode seen on many arcade games.

But others seem to suggest that Mystique thought it were indeed offering legitimate adult content rather than just teenage titillation. Again from the Mystique manuals:

> We at Mystique feel that it's time for video games and their adult players to come out of the closet, away from the kids, and deal with ADULT fantasies. After all, grownups have been known to be imaginative and competitive, as well as have fantasies.

These games may not be particularly noteworthy as culture, as games, or even as porn. But they do have historical interest, and they show us how flexible the commercial game environment of the early 1980s really was. And perhaps most startling, they represent a large percentage of the commercial marketplace for sex games in all eras, at least in the West.

Things are quite different in Japan, where cultural tolerance for sexually explicit materials is quite different from North America and Europe. While Western-style pornography exists in Japan, the country also supports another sort of adult material known as *hentai*. The term translates literally as "strange appearance," but more colloquially it simply means "pervert." As a form of pornography, *hentai* refers more specifically to sexually explicit comics and animation. Given common themes like tentacle erotica (tentacled creatures or monsters copulating with humans), *loli-con* (prepubescent girls), and *futanari* (hermaphroditic sex acts), Westerners often find *hentai* deeply disturbing compared with our comparatively "normal" pornography. But in Japan these forms are so ordinary as to seem almost humdrum.

The Japanese obsession with technology allowed *hentai* to make its way into videogames in a far more widespread fashion than has ever been the case in the West. Some of these games are much tamer than the *hentai* name would suggest. The most popular sort is known as *bishōjo* games, or "pretty girl games." Within this designation are several types, of various levels of explicitness. In the *ren'ai* game, or dating sim, players manage a male protagonist who must converse with a variety of girls in hopes of courting one. Dating sims are often completely nonsexual.

The more explicit variety of *bishōjo* is known as *erogē*, a shortening of the anglicized *erotic game*. Like dating sims, *erogē* are more like interactive novels and less like Mystique's sex action games or Lowe's adult adventure games. In addition to courtship, *erogē* often involve stripping games and sex simulations.

Games are just one aspect of a thriving and unfamiliar pornographic marketplace in Japan, one that most Westerners know little about. But because videogames enjoy such strong export from Japan, *hentai* games sometimes find their way stateside, where they're welcomed with even greater controversy than the comparatively tame and familiar hidden sex act in *Grand Theft Auto*.

The most explosive of these controversies surrounded *RapeLay*, an example of one of the many *erogē* that litter the Japanese marketplace. The game would disturb even the most stalwart of porno buffs—in it, the player stalks a girl on a subway platform and then molests her inside the crowded railcar. The game, which was never generally available in the United States anyway, made headlines when New York City Council Speaker Christine Quinn called for its boycott.[5]

Quinn's reaction is understandable, but it also misconstrues the social context for the game. The critic Leigh Alexander explains:

> The premise here is that a wealthy man is out for revenge against the schoolgirl who had him jailed as a *chikan*, or subway pervert. The epidemic of chikan is an enormous problem in Japan, particularly in major cities, where trains are so crowded that it's easy for predators to conceal their crimes. In Declan Hayes' 2005 book, *The Japanese Disease*, the author describes a community of salarymen who organize online "groping associations" and subscribe to publications that suggest ideal train lines and timetables for attacks.[6]

As Alexander notes, the game's violent scenario would still be considered so in Japan—but the context for comprehending even the very idea of this particular sort of perversion is almost entirely missing in the United States. Instead of banning a game that circulates only on the black market anyway, Alexander suggests that the underage *lolicon*-style *erogē*, which can be purchased quite easily in the United States, might be a better target for our outrage.

Nondigital forms of pornography circulate between cultures, but the digitizable or digitally native media have become much more portable thanks to the easy access of the Internet. While cultural conventions will always make any unfamiliar, foreign habit feel alien, the taboos on sex make discoveries like *RapeLay* even more startling for the unprepared. Though affront may certainly be justified, it's also worth turning that lens back on ourselves. For some cultures, the idea of a videogame featuring a man ejaculating from a roof might also seem fatally improprietous. Here a new purpose for playable pornography suggests itself: perhaps one use of videogame porn is not to titillate at all but to give us a defamiliarized and uncomfortable experience of the various logics of perversion that stimulate other human beings.

16 Exercise

Exercise is boring. We hate doing it, and we make excuses to avoid it. And when we do exercise, we usually try to drown it out with something more pleasant. On neighborhood sidewalks, joggers use iPods to make runs feel shorter and less lonely. Behind the glass windows of gyms, members stare at television screens as they wait for their elliptical machines to signal the end of a workout. We know we ought to exercise, but we wish it were less miserable to do so.

Unlike music and television, all videogame experiences require physical action. Not much action, in most cases, but action nonetheless. "Exergames" hope to make the interactive demands of videogames greater, such that they might reach the levels and rates of activity required for a workout while replacing sedentary leisure activity with active leisure activity. Instead of sitting in front of the television idle, mouth agape, we might step-to with *Dance Dance Revolution* or jump around with *Eye Toy: Kinetic*. Most of the games we celebrate for their exercise potential offer compelling entertainment experiences that also encourage (or better, demand) physical activity. And studies have coupled exergame play to measurable physical effects, from simple weight loss to cardiovascular health.[1]

But all of these games and the studies that laud them celebrate the exercise potential of games divorced from any cultural context in which exercise might happen naturally. And this division poses a problem. The sidewalk job and the office gym succeed not only because they offer a place to run but also because they afford a credible and familiar social context in which to do so.

< 110 >

There was a time when we didn't have to think so much about exercise. We tilled our own fields and slaughtered our own pigs. We churned our own butter and reaped our own squash or onions or potatoes. Getting through the winter offered physical challenge enough, and we worried more about disease than about fitness. Exercise was an accident of necessity.

In developed societies, most individuals are freed from the daily imposition of finding enough sustenance for the next day or week. We're able to reinvest that time in intellectual, spiritual, or material pursuits. But even early high-density societies preserved physical fitness as an important trait, more intertwined with daily life. Sport is one way organized societies developed their physical attributes, and sports in the ancient world were often tied to ritual and social values such as sacrifice, war, and individualism. Contests of physical skill like archery or footraces might just as easily have marked celebrations of mourning as they would contests of might. Exercise was still a by-product of the limited automation of daily life, but it was also a ritual practice.

In contemporary society, when we think of sport we usually think of spectator sport, like football or boxing matches. These activities probably share more in common with arena fighting, like ancient Roman gladiatorial combat, and carnival contests, like medieval English Shrovetide football, than they do with everyday ritual. Such sports were primarily intended for entertainment and spectacle, roles they still play.

Today, exercise is a major concern thanks to the so-called diseases of affluence like diabetes, heart disease, and obesity. We think of exercise as a way to compensate for increased use of cars, increased leisure, and greater inactivity at work. And so exercise has become reparation. Morning jogging and afternoon trips to the gym compensate for days at the computer and evenings in front of the TV. These kinds of exercises are stripped of the ceremonial or cultural features that once defined physically intensive work and sport. Like so many other aspects of industrial society, we have found ways to measure our exercise so as to maximize

performance and minimize time. Perhaps some business colleagues still review the day's business deals over a game of squash,
but by and large, we spin our legs on our exercise bikes all alone,
iPod buds nestled in our ears, waiting for the timer to beep merci-
fully so we can stop. Exercise has become a chore that we somehow
must squeeze into our busy routines.

The obsession with exercise as enumerated personal physical
performance has become so widespread that even players themselves have adopted physical performance as a primary metric
for the success of these games. Mickey DeLorenzo (an ordinary
gamer, not a researcher) ran a "Wii Sports Experiment," in which
he played *Wii Sports* for a half hour daily and meticulously tracked
his weight, body mass index (BMI), resting heart rate, calories
burned, and body fat over six weeks.[2] As DeLorenzo's experiment
testifies, the Wii seems to be a viable exercise platform thanks
to its games' demand for gestural interaction. Nintendo's early
ads for the system showed players of all ages jumping around in
front of their televisions, performing exactly the kinds of informal
physical exercise that proponents of exergames celebrate.

But exercise is not merely a measurable physiological outcome. Even if videogames might help us count and burn calories,
they also offer an opportunity to change the way we experience
or reflect on our world. In this respect, I was more than a little
amused when I unlocked the exercise level built into *Wario Ware:
Smooth Moves*, the Wii version of the popular franchise of tiny
"microgames." Dr. Crygor, the series's mad scientist, reveals his
latest invention, a thinning machine. At the start of the game, a
fatsuit-encased version of me (with accurate head taken from the
Mii avatar I had assigned to my game file) enters the contraption
and the games commence. Unlike normal *Wario Ware* play, the
player always gets a chance to play twenty microgames no matter
his or her performance, the implied goal of each to exercise as
much as possible. Performance is measured in an invented unit of
energy, the "kelorie," and the more/harder/faster the player works
in each microgame, the more kelories he or she burns.

It's unclear if Nintendo intended Crygor's diet game to offer a legitimate exercise experience, but I took it as a biting satire of exercise in general and videogame exercise in particular: every absurd gesture, from balloon inflating to nose picking, has been quantified in Wario's invented units. After the player completes the microgames, he or she is ejected from Crygor's device and deflated in accordance with his or her kelories burned. The experience exposes the inhumanity of exergames. Videogame-induced movements, it turns out, are no more inherently inspiring than exercise bikes or Stairmasters. *Wario Ware*'s microgames are cute and quirky, but their novelty quickly fades, and Wario's characteristic end-of-session cackle becomes the gracious alarm of a new kind of countdown timer.

Compare this experience with another popular videogame that also requires physical input: *Guitar Hero*. To be sure, the amount of physical exertion expended when strumming a plastic guitar is assuredly lower than that used when jumping and flailing with a Wii remote—but just getting players up off the couch counts as an accomplishment. Much of *Guitar Hero*'s success comes from its effective simulation of the jam session, the garage band act, and rock superstar performance. Add a friend and you can compete or you can collaborate. By simulating a ritual activity like the jam session, *Guitar Hero* also becomes an abstract instance of that ritual itself.

When played without the heart monitors, scales, and BMI calculators, *Wii Sports* offers a similar experience. The rituals of sport as competitive social practice remain strong among amateurs who golf, play tennis, box, or bowl for real. Sure, some of us may hit the course, the court, the ring, or the alley for exercise, but we return to these places thanks to the social rituals that surround them: everything from the locker room taunts to the scorecard handicap. When we play *Wii Sports* with one or two friends or family members, we re-create micro-environments that mimic the golf course or the bowling alley. One thing I notice in particular while playing these games is how I fill the time between turns: sometimes I watch, but just as frequently I read, or write email, or chat with other people in the room until, "Oh, is it my turn again?" This sort of social environment is similar to that of the neighborhood basketball court, the golf course, or the bowling alley.

Exergames must inspire their players to move. But they also must inspire their players to *want* to move. In doing so, these games both adopt existing rituals and practices from other domains, like sports, and establish new ones unique to videogames. *Guitar Hero* and *Wii Sports* are successful examples of ritual-bound physical games, but they borrow their rituals entirely from other domains. Even successful exergames like *Dance Dance Revolution* offer only transitional examples of developed videogame exercise rituals: *DDR* on the home console completely erases the complex social dance performance practices of the arcade game—*DDR* experts perform in public to peacock; the exercise is just serendipity. *Wario Ware,* by contrast, creates a new and unusual fictional context atop its movement-oriented gameplay, one that inspires a group to laugh and perform rather than to compete.

Games can craft individual rituals, too. When we do exercise alone, we often do it on the go: by walking or jogging. Nowadays, most people have a powerful computer with them all the time, in the form of a mobile phone. The health insurance provider Humana created the iPhone title *GoldWalker,* an adventure game in which the player takes the role of a forty-niner in the Sierras during the California gold rush. It sports the usual trappings of an adventure game—buying equipment, selling spoils, avoiding bandits. But the game is about prospecting, and prospecting involves searching for possible sources of gold. *GoldWalker* takes advantage of this fictional opportunity and requires the player to walk between prospecting locations in the adventure. This isn't simulated walking but *literal* walking; the device acts as a pedometer, which the player can hold in a hand, pocket, or purse to detect movement. On reaching a destination (in both the real and the virtual worlds), the adventure continues.

The power of devices like the iPhone notwithstanding, a fancy computer isn't even necessary. *Arukotch* is a tamagotchi-like virtual pet embedded in a pedometer. Tamagotchi are already portable, and most even resemble a simple mechanical pedometer anyway. The "pet" in *Arukotch* is a "shy girl waiting for a proposal from a cute boy."[3] The more steps the player takes, the more "healthy and beautiful" she becomes. Items like cell phones and gifts also reveal themselves as you walk more. These items can aid in wooing the promised cute boy. Saccharine though the concept may be, the simple coupling of gameplay to a small, portable toy offers a more likely ritual activity than does hauling a bulky piece of equipment into the living room. Indeed, Nike and Apple have made just that assumption, investing heavily in the Nike+ system, which connects a sensor in the runner's shoe to a program on an iPod or iPhone the jogger carries (a newer iPhone version doesn't require the shoe insert but uses the device's internal GPS sensor).[4] The results don't integrate with an adventure game like *GoldWalker*; instead, the system allows joggers to upload statistics from their runs to the Nike website, where players can challenge friends to match their times or otherwise seek encouragement and competition.

Physical controllers for home play have been around for over twenty-five years, but they have only ever occupied the fringes of the marketplace: Atari's never-released "Puffer" exerbike controller, Amiga's 1982 Joyboard, LJN's 1988 Roll 'n Rocker. As more physical input devices have hit the market, including the Microsoft Kinect and Sony Move, it is tempting to assume that videogame play will *automatically* become more active, more viable, and therefore more valuable as exercise. But once the novelty has worn off, players will find shortcuts absent strong social and cultural contexts in which to play their videogames actively. The Wii, it turns out, affords far more slothful play than its traditional controller-bound competitors (try it yourself; you can play *The Legend of Zelda: Twilight Princess* slouched back in your sofa, hands at your sides. Just wiggle the Wii remote hand to swing your sword). To incite long-lasting, highly motivated physical activity, exergames do more than issue demands for repetitive physical gestures that produce latent exercise. In addition, they both simulate and create the social rituals that make us want to be physically active, whether through computers or portable devices, and whether alone or with others.

17
Work

When we encounter a work in any medium, our experiences with it can influence how we think about our real lives. But for many players, a videogame is something one does *outside* everyday life, disconnected from it, safe, otherworldly. Playing a game is different from sorting digital photos, filing business receipts, or responding to emails.

Even serious games maintain a distance from ordinary life. A corporate training game or an advergame might be crafted for a purpose outside the game—for example, learning how to implement a fast-food franchise's customer service process or exploring the features and functions of a new mobile phone. But even so, playing the game isn't the same thing as fielding customer complaints at the taco hut or managing appointments in the mobile calendar. Doing those things requires leaving the game and re-entering the real world.

There is power in using games as an "act apart," to use one of Johan Huizinga's terms for the separateness of play.[1] When games invite us inside them, they also underwrite experimentation, ritual, role-playing, and risk taking that might be impossible or undesirable in the real world. When videogames take over our television screens or black out our computer desktops, they act as portals to alternate realities. When we play games, we temporarily interrupt and set aside ordinary life.

But that's not really anything unusual. We do the same thing when we curl up in an armchair with a novel, or when the lights go down in a theater, or when we plug in our earbuds on the commuter train.

< 117 >

But, in other media, immersion in a world apart is only one of many modalities. We don't just read novels, we also read road signs and sales reports and postal mail. We don't just watch film or television, we also watch security monitors and focus group recordings and weather reports. We don't just listen to music, we also listen to telephone ringtones and train chimes and lullabies. In these cases, when we interact with the writing, or the moving images, or the music, we *simultaneously* perform or experience an action, be it work, play, or something mundane and in-between.

Philosophers and linguists sometimes distinguish between different types of speech. One such distinction contrasts speech acts that describe things from those that do things. The philosopher of language J. L. Austin gave the term *constative* to speech acts that describe things.[2] Most ordinary speech falls into this category: "Roses are red, violets are blue"; "I wish I were Zorro"; "Finishing all his kale so reviled young Ernesto that he lost his interest in the éclair." These acts describe the world but don't act on it. A *performative* is a term for speech acts that do things themselves when they're uttered. The classic example of the performative is the cleric or magistrate's declaration, "I now pronounce you man and wife." In this case, the utterance itself performs the action of initiating the marriage union. Other examples are promises and apologies, christenings and wagers, firing and sentencing. "I promise to come home by midnight"; "I dub thee Sir Wilbur"; "You're fired!"; "I bet you $100 I can beat 'Through the Fire and Flames' on Expert." When we utter such statements, the act of speaking itself issues the commitment or regret, the naming or the bet.

In every videogame, players' actions make the game work: tilting an analog stick to move Crash Bandicoot; pressing the "Y" button to make Niko Bellic carjack a Comet sports coupe; strumming the fret of a *Rock Band* guitar to puppet the on-screen guitarist. Such is the definition of interactivity, after all.

But there's also another, rarer kind of gameplay action, one that performs some action outside the game at the same time as it does so in the game. The performative offers one way to understand such actions. In these cases, things a player does when playing take on a meaning in the game, but they also literally do something in the world beyond the game and its players.

On first blush, exercise games seem like an obvious example. In a game like *Wii Fit,* the player exerts physical effort to play, such as balancing on one leg or doing a push-up, the aggregate results of which improve his or her physical condition over time. The same is true for physical performance games. In *Dance Dance Revolution,* the player moves around in a way that not only approximates dancing but also demands physical exertion. Such games clearly accentuate the aerobic potential of videogames and their immediate effects on the body.

But exergame actions affect only the player, and only in an incremental, nearly invisible way. When a bride says "I do" at the pulpit, she enters a new state of commitment completely and immediately. But when she performs a push-up on her Wii Balance Board, no particular state of fitness arises; it happens little by little, over time, in ways that each push-up can't fully explain. In Austin's terms, a performative has to be *complete* to be considered an earnest one (he calls them "happy performatives").[3] Stronger examples of performative physical interfaces would act on something more completely, and they would also have the potential to act on more than just the player himself or herself.

Consider the *PainStation,* a game installation created by the German artists Volker Morawe and Tilman Reiff in 2001. *PainStation* is a variant of *Pong* built into a cocktail-style arcade cabinet. Two players compete by controlling a paddle with a knob in the usual fashion. The other hand must rest on a metal sensor, completing a circuit to enable the game. When a player misses a ball, it contacts a pain symbol corresponding with one of three different types of pain: heat, electric shock, and flagellation. As each power-up passes the goal line, the corresponding pain is inflicted on the player through a heat element, electric circuit, and leather lash built into the table. The first to remove his or her hand from the sensor loses the game.

Morawe and Reiff have called *PainStation* a videogame adaptation of the duel.[4] Although the outcome is less dire than a bout of pistols, the *PainStation* means business; a web search reveals a cornucopia of ghastly injuries sustained by *PainStation* combatants. Like the duel, *PainStation* is a test of honor or a challenge of champions. Its participants literally perform violence on an opponent through the game. These are games that themselves *do work,* that enact *performative play.*

Another place to find performative play is in mixed-reality games that couple computational interaction to real-world interaction in deliberate ways. There are many genres of such games: mobile games, ubiquitous games, pervasive games, alternate reality games (ARGs) are among them. But not all of them necessarily involve performative play. A handset game played in a train or a puzzle game played by GPS hardly alters the state of the world through play alone. The ones that do focus on game actions whose meaning and effect are layered, such that the same act has an in-game and out-of-game function and outcome. Furthermore, the meaning of the one often seems to inform or determine that of the other.

Cruel 2 B Kind, a game I created with Jane McGonigal, is a mobile phone–controlled real-world adaptation of the popular live-action role-playing game *Assassin.* Instead of using water pistols or the other faux weapons common to *Assassin, Cruel 2 B Kind*'s weapons are acts of kindness: compliment a person's footwear; wish him or her a pleasant day; perform a serenade for him or her. The game is played in groups within bounded urban environments among pedestrian populations. Since the participants are not revealed before the game, part of the experience involves deducing who is and who is not playing. In the process, it's common to compliment or serenade ordinary folks going about their daily business. In such cases, well wishes still function normally, bringing surprising but harmless pleasantry to people caught in the game's crossfire.

Another mixed-reality game with performative results is the iTVS-sponsored *World without Oil,* an ARG about a global oil crisis, created by Ken Eklund and McGonigal. To play, participants created stories about their imagined strategies to get through daily life during an oil shortfall. Some wrote or recorded hypothetical accounts, while others literally enacted oil-saving strategies like planting community gardens or starting carpools. Doing so contributes to oil conservation in real ways, even if small ones.

The Carnegie Mellon computer scientists Manuel Blum and Luis von Ahn's human computation games offer a very different example.[5] The best known is probably the *ESP Game,* in which two remote players see the same image and try to guess words the other would use to describe them. As the game finds a match, it not only rewards points but also stores the matching terms as descriptive tags for the images. Google has even licensed the game (as the "Google Image Labeler") to train its image search algorithm.[6] Von Ahn calls them "games with a purpose," or "gwap" for short. Other gwap games work similarly: *Tag a Tune* for identifying music, *Squigl* for identifying object positions within images.

In *Cruel 2 B Kind* and *World without Oil,* the reality mixed into the game is physicality. In gwap games, the mixed reality is labor. Their gameplay performs a kind of work that's hard for computers but easy for humans. When players partake of the *ESP Game,* they perform the tagging of images directly and simultaneously with every move in the game. Here gameplay resembles the performative act of christening a ship or a building.

That said, there's something "unhappy" in Austin's sense about gwaps' performative play: unlike *World without Oil* or *PainStation,* they fail to reveal and contextualize the meaning of their actions. Players may have some sense that the games contribute to image or music tagging, but they don't understand the implications of such actions in the way they understand promises and wagers when they perform such speech acts. This defect raises ethical concerns as much as formal ones. When a game performs an action without the player's understanding of its implications, it confuses performativity and exploitation. "I do" is a meaningful performative utterance because bride, groom, and witnesses all fully understand its implications. But the *ESP Game* veils the possible implications of image tags, for example, as tools for surveillance as much as for image searches. Though von Ahn may style them "games with a purpose," a purpose alone is not enough to describe performative play. Context and convention are also required.

Ethical matters notwithstanding, exercise, kindness, oil conservation, and metadata gathering are far more dramatic actions than many things done through other media. Restroom signs and rearview cameras are useful tools, but they're also mundane ones; people need to find toilets and avoid tricycles. Performative play in games can address more mundane activities like these as well.

Consider enterprise solutions start-up Seriosity's product *Attent*. Here's the concept: we all get too much email, which reduces productivity. In large organizations, much of this email is sent internally. The attention cost of receiving email doesn't match that of sending it. Things just get worse as the recipients become more senior, and therefore their time more valuable. Time management isn't the answer, less email is. And one way to reduce the email people receive is to make it more precious to send.

Attent tries to do exactly this, making email more expensive to send, or at least making people more deliberate about how they do so. Since attention cost rises with seniority and expertise, email can be recast as an attention game: the CEO's attention costs more than the junior manager's, so the latter should have to "pay more" to get the attention of the former. And likewise, senior executives would take a request from junior ones more seriously if the latter had to spend more of their scarce attention capital to obtain it.

Attent turns attention into capital, literally, via a scrip currency called serios. Workers can get serios by accepting email with attached payments, or companies can choose to dole it out in other ways as incentives or rewards. *Attent* works as a plug-in for the popular corporate email client Microsoft Outlook, so it's possible for workers to track their credits along with their calendar and even to sort email by its value in serios rather than by date.

Office politics feels like a game because it involves many unpredictable, intersecting decisions that recombine in complex ways. Office work often involves strategy and planning, but it all happens behind the scenes, off the time clock. *Attent* puts that work back on the books, but reveals rather than hides the social rules that drive office work. For example, a group of lower-level workers can aggregate their attention capital by amassing serios-filled emails to one another, whose loot a representative can then use to get attention up the chain. *Attent* tightly couples the workplace and the workplace game, such that "moves" in the game correspond closely to direct action in the workplace.

The Grocery Game offers another example of more mundane performative play. A web-based service provides data on the cheapest goods at local supermarkets, as well as tips on saving money on groceries through bulk purchase strategies. The goal of the game is to reduce one's family grocery costs as much as possible. Implied subgoals like turning a $100 grocery bill into a $5 one through extremely efficient uses of coupons and specials drive competition and community. In *The Grocery Game,* the act of playing, shopping, and saving compresses, such that the first action enacts the latter two. Through tightly coupled performative play, *Attent* and *The Grocery Game* show how some games have more in common with doorbells and exit placards than immersive fantasy worlds.

Tomy's Banquest turns *The Grocery Game* on its head, making the savings drive the play rather than vice versa. Banquest is a piggy bank for kids, with a tiny digital role-playing game built into the front. Coins dropped into the bank become savings in the ordinary sense, but they also get translated into gold in the game, which can be used to buy items like weapons and armor. Here the performative play is even more tightly coupled with the action it performs: filling the in-game wallet simultaneously fills the real one. And kids still get to spend the money they save.

What does playing a game do to people in the world? In the case of entertainment games, such a question is often understood to inquire about the effects of violence on players or about how players find and evaluate meaning in games. In training, advertising, and learning games, the question asks how players take knowledge they learned in a game and apply it in their daily lives. The motivational (and sometimes compulsive) aspects of games suggest other ways gameplay can influence behavior. But such matters cover only part of the intersection between our game lives and our ordinary lives.

In speech, performatives function because people understand both the meaning of the words they utter and the actions they cause. Austin suggests that performatives make conscious actions explicit; this is why making a promise works. Likewise, in games that feature performative mechanics, the player knows both the performance and the play, and their implications are simultaneous and immediate.

Performativity in discourse couples speech to real-world action rather than to representation. Performativity in videogames couples gameplay to real-world action. Performative gameplay describes mechanics that change the state of the world through play actions themselves, rather than by inspiring possible future actions through coercion or reflection. But there's an important distinction to note between performative play and more-generic real-world effects. As examples like *Wii Fit* and the *ESP Game* demonstrate, performativity is a special kind of play that for which outcome alone is an insufficient criterion. In addition, the player must develop a conscious understanding of the purpose, effect, and implications of his or her actions, so that they bear meaning as cultural conditions, not just instrumental contrivances.

18 Habituation

Here's a game design aphorism you may have heard before: a game, so it goes, ought to be "easy to learn and hard to master."

This axiom is so frequently repeated because it purports to hold the key to a powerful outcome: an *addicting game,* one people want to play over and over again once they've started, and in which starting is smooth and easy. It's an adage most frequently applied to casual games, but it's also used to describe complex games of deep structure and emergent complexity.

In the modern era, this familiar design guideline comes from coin-op. The aphorism is often attributed, in a slightly different form, to Atari's founder, Nolan Bushnell. In his honor, the concept has earned the title "Bushnell's Law" or "Nolan's Law":

All the best games are easy to learn and difficult to master.
They should reward the first quarter and the hundredth.

Bushnell learned this lesson firsthand when his first arcade cabinet *Computer Space,* a coin-op adaptation of the early PDP-1 videogame *Space War!,* failed to meet commercial expectations. *Computer Space* was complex, with two buttons for ship rotation, one for thrust, and another one for fire. While the same layout would eventually enjoy incredible success in the coin-op *Asteroids,* four identical buttons with different functions was too much for the arcade player of 1971.

Pong was supposedly inspired by this failure, a game so simple it could be taught in a single sentence: *Avoid missing ball for high score.* It seems so obvious, doesn't it? Games that are easy to start

< 125 >

up the first time but also offer long-term appeal have the potential to become classics. Except for one problem: the "easy to learn, hard to master" aphorism doesn't mean what you think it does.

Bushnell's eponymous law notwithstanding, the design values of quick pickup and long-term play surely didn't originate with him. Poker is another game that commonly enjoys the description. The same is true for classic board games like Go, chess, and Othello. Indeed, the famous board game inventor George Parker apparently adopted a different version of Bushnell's Law in the late nineteenth century. From Philip Orbanes's history of Parker Brothers:

> Each game must have an exciting, relevant theme and be easy enough for most people to understand. Finally, each game should be so sturdy that it could be played time and again, without wearing out.[1]

Note the subtle differences between Bushnell's take and Parker's. Parker isn't especially concerned with the *learnability* of a game, just that it deal with a familiar topic in a comprehensible way. A century hence, time is more precious (or less revered), and simplifying the act of learning a game became Bushnell's focus. Still, something more complex than familiar controls or simple instructions is at work here.

It makes sense: *Pong* isn't easy to learn, at all, for someone who has never played or seen racquet sports. Without knowledge of such sports, the game would seem just as alien as a space battle around a black hole.

As it happens, table tennis became popular in Victorian England around the same time Parker began creating games seriously. It offered an indoor version of tennis, a popular lawn sport among the upper class, played with ad hoc accoutrements in libraries or conservatories.

Both ordinary tennis and its indoor table variety had enjoyed over a century of continuous practice by the time Bushnell and the Atari engineer Al Alcorn popularized their videogame adaptation of the sport (itself a revision of two earlier efforts, Willy Higginbotham's *Tennis for Two* and Ralph Baer's "Brown Box," which later became the Magnavox Odyssey). *Pong* offers quick pickup not because it's easier to learn than *Computer Space* (although that was also true) but because it draws on familiar conventions from that sport. Or better, *Pong* is "easy to learn" precisely because it assumes the basic rules and function of a familiar cultural practice.

Familiarity is thus the primary property of the game, not learnability; it's familiarity that makes something easy to learn. It's what makes "Avoid missing ball" make any sense in the first place. *Wii Sports* offers a similar lesson. The broad success of the Wii console comes in no small part from the effectiveness of this launch title. *Wii Sports* is really just *Pong* warmed over, offering simple abstractions of well-known sports that are themselves quite complex to learn, but which large populations have managed to understand over time. We become habituated to them.

What about casual games? *Tetris* isn't really easy to learn either. Sure, it offers simple controls and a comprehensible goal, but nothing about those controls or that goal is obvious or intuitive; they are not inherently familiar ideas. But the game's tiles, called tetrominoes, those *are* familiar. Tile games find their roots in dominoes, an ancient game, one millennium old in its earliest forms. Polyominoes (a shape made of a certain number of connected squares; *Tetris* pieces use four) have been common elements of puzzles since the early twentieth century, most frequently found in tiling puzzles (like pentominoes) or assembly puzzles (like tangrams).

Tetris cleverly combines both the assembly and the tiling varieties of polyomino puzzles, asking the player to construct a small subtiled region (a line) by making micro-assemblies of two or three blocks. Rather than place blocks, the player manipulates them as they fall.

As all of these examples suggest, habituation builds on prior conventions. *Pong* builds on table tennis, which builds on tennis, which builds on racquets. *Tetris* builds on pentominoes, which builds on dominoes, which builds on early games of dice and bones.

Games can also produce their own conventions, which become familiar enough to be adopted later in the same way that *Pong* adopts table tennis. The falling tetrominoes of *Tetris,* for example, inspire the falling blocks of *Columns* or *Dr. Mario* or *Klax*—games that make modifications to familiar conventions from earlier games as they congeal.

Likewise, the familiarity of subjects helps apologize for unfamiliarity of form. Parker's early game Banking (1883) built on players' basic knowledge of financial practices. Popular casual games in the vein of *Diner Dash* do the same, relying on a player's familiarity with waitressing, hairdressing, or other professions. No matter the case, the result is important: the maxim "easy to learn" is misunderstood. Mechanical simplicity is less important than conceptual familiarity.

So much for "easy to use." What about "hard to master?"

Some games are profound enough to deserve the provocation toward mastery, but not many. Chess and Go do by virtue of complexity and emergence: they're games that offer such rich and intricate variation that only careful, long-term study can produce proficiency. This is why the concept of a chess master means something more than simply someone who just plays a lot. Chess and Go are games for which mastery is definitively "hard."

At the 2009 Game Developers Conference, the designer and educator Tracy Fullerton observed that the very hard mastery of such games inspires less able players by tracing the edges of the game's beauty.[2] We might call this the terrain of *sublime mastery*. And there's indeed a fearful wonder in this territory. But it's also a weird mastery, one that sits at the fringes of a game, alienating as much as it inspires. The standard rationale for mastery makes appeals to the depth of a game, suggesting that the value of its design cannot be expended in only a few sessions but would require innumerable replays, perhaps theoretically infinite ones, to reveal all its secrets. The problem is, sublime mastery is usually desirable only as an ideal, not as an experience.

It's no secret that Bushnell was a fan of Go. "Atari," after all, is a technical term from that game. So it's easy to assume that the "difficult to master" portion of Bushnell's Law refers to NP-hard problems of the Go variety. But the second portion of his proverb suggests a different meaning.

That a game should "reward the first quarter as well as the hundredth" (this was the era of the coin-op) suggests nothing about the cosmic intricacy of a game like Go. Instead, it suggests that a game ought to produce allure many times. Bushnell's Law makes no claim about the kind of appeal a game ought to make on the tenth or hundredth playing, nor if that allure ought to be entirely different or new every time. Likewise, Parker's design techniques make no claims about mastery either. He does, however, clarify one sort of appeal a game might offer over time.

Parker is concerned with material, not conceptual, durability, when he says that a game should be able to be played time and time again. While such resilience does imply some reason to want to play again, it does not imply any kind of invitation toward mastery whatsoever, whether practical or sublime. The game's allure must simply inspire multiple plays, not necessarily multiple unique plays, or multiple plays approaching an ideal. As Orbanes explains, Parker Brothers valued durability. "Make it last" became a company creed.[3] Indeed, the matter of quality of material and manufacture helped make Parker Brothers games appealing as artifacts, not just as games.

Like any craft object, a board or card game can create different levels of physical attachment. The design of Monopoly, with its modernist typography, winsome illustrations, and forged tokens, creates a game of material appeal, one that produces pleasure in the holding, viewing, and possessing as well as in the playing. Monopoly becomes a place we want to go back to, just as does *Bioshock*'s Rapture or *World of Warcraft*'s Azeroth. The fact that we can enjoy arguing over who gets to be the car or the dog in a game of *Monopoly* is just as important as the appeal of the game's mechanics (which indeed are far more rapidly exhausted than those of Go).

Similarly, *Pong* does not reward the hundredth quarter through emergent complexity. Instead, it rewards that quarter through social context. In the 1970s coin-ops were mostly found in places like bars and bowling alleys, and indeed the game borrowed the very same context that makes tavern games like darts and pool appealing: one can play them with friends while drinking. Sure, one can get better at *Pong* like one can get better at eight ball, but the real purpose of these games is to offer a chance to commune with (or mock) one's mates over brews.

Most people don't really care if they master *Pong* or pool—or *Tetris* or chess, for that matter. Instead, people like to be conversant in these games so that they can incorporate them into various practices, moving beyond the phase of learning the basics and on to the phase of using the games for purposes beyond their mechanics alone. Indeed, idealizing the sublime mastery of the sort the chess master or pool shark pursues may even serve as an *undesirable* characteristic for ordinary players.

In 1906 the *New York Times* reported a precipitous decline in the popularity of racquets, predicting its inevitable supplanting by squash, thanks to the latter's cheaper cost and easier mastery. Said Peter Latham, then eighteen-year reigning champion of the sport, "Racquets is far more difficult to master than squash or court tennis. I think racquets will remain where it is, while squash will continue to grow in popularity."[4] The supplanting of racquets by squash suggests that a low, rather than a high, ceiling to mastery might offer greater rather than less appeal. As in the case of chess or Go, the relative difficulty of the former sport made it seem inaccessible rather than appealing.

That's great for early twentieth-century indoor sports, but what does it matter for twenty-first-century videogames? Consider a casual downloadable game like *Zuma*. Like many casual games, *Zuma* offers a free trial, in this case one that's three levels long.

Games of this sort suffer from conversion rates as low as 1 percent (from trial downloads to full purchases).[5]

We might conclude that for games like *Zuma,* the trial offers enough habituation to serve a gratifying purpose for most players. Becoming adept at the three or so levels of *Zuma's* trial requires limited skill, drive, or persistence. It's inevitable, really. The demo is gratifying enough as it is, habituating players to a certain level of performance they're able to accomplish easily. This is not mastery at all; in the case of *Zuma,* the habitual activity of repeated play is likely to relate to biding time or zoning out more than it is to encourage increased performance. Arguably, the same is true for *Tetris.* Just imagine if "free demo levels" had been the norm when that game was released in 1986. Who would have needed anything more?

Given their numerical scores, high-score lists, achievements, and myriad other ways to measure performance tangibly, it's true that videogames, board games, tavern games, and sports sometimes do invite us to pursue certain accomplishments. But more frequently, we feel compelled to return to games that we've habituated ourselves to for other reasons. *Airport Mania* lets players have a go at air traffic controlling for a few minutes. *Tetris* affords a feeling of control and organization in a world of entropy. Like "easy to learn," "hard to master" turns out to be a rare secondary property of games, one most frequently left for the pro ballplayers, chess masters, and card sharks—all specialists, not generalists, as the casual games lore would have us believe.

Here's a surprising notion that might explain both familiarity and habituation in games: *catchiness.*

Think about a catchy song, the kind you can't get out of your head when you hear it. How does that happen? The reason songs stick with us is unclear, but some researchers have called it a "cognitive itch," a stimulus that creates a missing idea that our brains can't help but fill in.[6] Whether the brain science is true or not isn't really important; it offers a helpful metaphor through which to pose another question: what causes the itch?

Paul Barsom, a Penn State professor of music composition, suggests several factors that seem to aid in making a song catchy.[7] Conveniently, they correspond well to my rereading of Bushnell's Law above.

One is familiarity. Says Barsom, "A certain familiarity—similarity to music one already knows—can play a role [in making a song catchy]. Unfamiliar music doesn't connect well." It makes sense: the effort required to grasp a new musical concept, genre, or approach makes the higher-order work of just feeling the music hard to access.

Familiarity relates to another of Barsom's observations: repetition. Catchy songs often have a "hook," a musical phrase where the majority of the catchy payload resides. Indeed, the itch usually lasts only a few bars, sometimes annoyingly so.

But games rely on small atoms of interaction even more so than do songs. The catchy part of a game repeats more innately than does a song's chorus. In *Tetris* it's the fitting together of tetrominoes. In *Diner Dash* it's the gratification of servicing a customer. In *Drop7* it's the mental calculation of a stone's position. It's also in such tiny refrains where these and other catchy games revisit familiar conventions.

Another property is what Barsom calls a "cultural connection." When a song attaches itself to an external concept, sensation, or idea, it seems to increase its ability to become catchy. The Beach Boys' catchy songs connected newfound ideas of summer and beach life to more complex themes of longing and desire. When Katy Perry sings about kissing a girl in the same year that witnesses controversial legislation about gay rights, she creates a less-charged mental space for mulling over such questions.

Cultural connections help habituate ideas. They give them form, acclimatizing listeners—or players—to the social contexts in which ideas might be used. In 1972 *Pong* introduced the world to the idea that computers were about to become machines for exploring ideas and interacting with people. In 2006 *Wii Sports* reactivated the den as a social space for families, recuperating the lost digital hearth of the Atari/Intellivision era. With music, we embody catchiness by running a song over in our heads or tapping a foot. With games, we embody catchiness by playing again, for specific reasons.

Game designers talk openly about how to make their games "more addicting," but "catchy" is certainly a better verbal frame than is "addicting." Indeed, why would anyone choose to call their craft "addicting," a descriptor we normally reserve for unpopular corporeal sins like nicotine? Why would we want game design to sound like drug dealing, the first "easy to use" hit opening a guileful Pandora's box of "hard mastery?" The rhetorical benefits of "catchiness" alone suggest its adoption. But more so, most people don't really *want* to make games that are "easy to learn and hard to master." A game that's easy to learn probably isn't a bad thing, but it doesn't get at the heart of the sort of appeal that leads to catchiness.

Many games are hard to master, and they're not the ones that normally earn the label of "casual." *Metal Gear Solid* is hard to master. So is *Mega Man 9*. Ditto *Ninja Gaiden*. These games are hard to master because they're punishingly difficult. Striving for a design that demands mastery isn't bad; it's just that it's not the goal served by the designs that adopt Bushnell's Law. Mastery, it turns out, is a highly specialized carrot that works only in extreme circumstances; indeed, the ludic sublime is probably a very rare terrain. Most of the time, creating habituation is enough: making players want to come back to visit your game, whether or not they want to eke out every morsel of performance from the thing.

Bushnell's Law is not useless or base, but it has been universally misunderstood. It doesn't explain the phenomenon we have assumed it does. Instead, it suggests that games can culture familiarity by constructing habitual experiences. They do so by finding receptors for familiar mechanics and tuning them slightly differently, so as to make those receptors resonate in a gratifyingly familiar way.

19 Disinterest

One year at the Electronic Entertainment Expo (E3) in Los Angeles, the U.S. Army hosted a spectacle of military excess outside the L.A. Convention Center's South Hall, to promote the new Special Forces edition of their popular title *America's Army*. As part of this spectacle, they offered passersby the opportunity to pose holding a large assault rifle next to a camouflaged Special Forces operative and a Humvee. In a nimble perversion of the tourist trap, the army even offered complimentary Polaroid photos of potential players (and recruits) posed for glorious combat.

Just like many spectacles, this performance benefited more than just the army. It served the industry as a whole, drawing general attention to videogames through the example of *America's Army*. Here gun porn and booth soldiers took the place of soft porn and booth babes, but to the same effect: to promote and reinforce the roles players want to occupy.

Reflecting on the experience, the critic Noah Wardrip-Fruin observed, "Most games offer variations on the fantasy of being a "gun/sword/spell-toting tough guy."[1] The Special Forces soldier, after all, is a role common to videogames, not just those produced by the army. If videogames place us in other people's shoes, those shoes are very often combat boots.

As videogames expand in scope and purpose, they offer players access to different sorts of fantasies. The almost unthinkable success of the United Nations World Food Programme's serious game *Food Force* underscores this promise. *Food Force* is a game about being a humanitarian. Yet few games, no matter if they're produced for education or entertainment, take on a slightly more

< 134 >

specific challenge: are there valid, even positive fantasies that also involve gun toting? Can games offer positive messages about carrying and using firearms?

One might point to the wealth of games, both in number and in dollars invested, that strip fantasy from military action. Games like *Full Spectrum Warrior* offer detailed depictions of military service that de-emphasize the discharge of weapons in favor of more "realistic" combat scenarios. No matter the case, these games still rely on the soldiering tough-guy fantasy, even if they present a soldiering tough-guy following the chain of command. But there's another candidate for novel gun fantasy, and perhaps a surprising one. It's a PlayStation game that bears the name and endorsement of the American gun lobby organization, the National Rifle Association.

NRA Gun Club is a target shooting game. It contains over one hundred firearms, all realistically modeled both in appearance and in operation, from discharge to reload. Players choose from around a dozen shooting challenges, from an indoor target range to an outdoor skeet field to a carnival shooting gallery.

As one might expect, the game adopts the conventions of the first-person shooter (FPS) genre. The player stands behind the firearm, or looks through a sight in some cases, taking aim at the center of a target. E3 previews of the game did not even seem to suggest considerable additional detail over traditional FPS gunplay, save the ability to hold one's breath when sighting to achieve a more accurate shot. Following common convention, players can play a kind of sportsman's "career" mode in which they become certified on a particular firearm in order to unlock new classes and new guns.

Many people—perhaps even avid players of brutal FPSs—may cringe at the very idea of an NRA-licensed game. For some, the endorsement is reason enough to shun *Gun Club*. For others, the NRA name may raise bitter memories of *Deer Hunter* and its cousins, titles that still sell much better than more highly crafted, nuanced games. The attentive cynic might even note that the game's publisher, Crave Entertainment, also published *The Bible*

Game, a Bible trivia game for Game Boy and PlayStation 2 primarily intended for children. God and Guns, a tagline that sometimes doubles as a foreign policy.

I would challenge such skeptics to look beyond preconceptions of the NRA and analyze this game on its own terms. For one part, it traces the organization's increasingly sophisticated approach to videogame-based public communication. This isn't the first NRA-endorsed videogame. Back in 2004 Interactive Sports Entertainment and Marketing created *NRA Varmint Hunter,* in which the player brandishes firearms against infestations of groundhogs and prairie dogs. Marketing materials for the game assured "realistic animal behavior" modeling, thanks to a collaboration with the Varmint Hunters Association. The game's splash screen depicted an unassuming prairie dog in the crosshairs of a long-range sight. The player even visited a bumpkinish general store to stock up on supplies.

Whatever preconceptions one might have about the NRA and its membership, *Varmint Hunter*'s developers clearly chose an unflattering characterization. With *NRA Gun Club,* the organization makes an important rhetorical turn away from the gun's reputation as an adornment of hayseeds, hicks, and yokels. In fact, the fetishization of guns in videogames of the last two decades may make *Gun Club* one of the most effective serious games of recent note, as it offers a fantasy of gunplay that stands in stark contrast to that of most popular media.

Reviews of *Varmint Hunter* were, to use the game review website Gamespot's official terminology, "abysmal."[2] One reviewer kind enough to score it "terrible" called it "very boring . . . and repetitive." Another called it "disastrous," asking, "what can you say about a game that shoots rodents? . . . trash it." One might attribute such a response to offense at the killing of innocent creatures, but a later comment reveals that the disaster is one of execution, not of conception: "The (simulated) reload time is super slow. . . . I mean, if you really want to shoot a vermit [*sic*] as fast as possible, you won't take 2 minutes to reload!!!!" *NRA Gun Club* fared no better—earning another "abysmal" rating and the back-handed praise, "Absolutely pure in its devotion to awfulness."[3]

It ought to be no surprise: anyone who actually has shot at a firing range knows just how slow-paced and even boring the activity really is. Perhaps the only sport of greater boredom between gestures is golf, yet at least that time can be filled with gossip or business dealings. Just as all golf videogames abstract the long stroll from ball to ball, all firearms games abstract the tedium of reloads and gun handling. But perhaps firing guns for marksmanship *ought to be* slow, arduous work. Merely holding a real gun is anything but fun—in my experience it's quite an anxious activity. The reality of a firearm's power is an overwhelming sensation, and a reminder of the seriousness of such weapons. Yet the representation of firearms in most videogames is exactly the opposite: it's one of celebration, of power fantasy, and of general inconsequence. I'm not referring to inconsequence in the act of shooting and killing, but of inconsequence in the mere act of holding a weapon capable of such feats.

By making firearms boring, *NRA Gun Club* might actually perform the rhetoric many have previously laughed off as politicking and fabrication: the responsible handling of firearms. One might even go so far as to say that *NRA Gun Club* owes most of its rhetorical power to the commercial FPS. The very obsession with the fantasy of gunplay common to commercial videogames creates an empty space in which the fantasy of responsible gun handling takes more coherent form than it might do in any other medium: at the end of the day, being a marksman might just not be very interesting.

Of course, *NRA Gun Club* says nothing about the organization's fervent support of hunting or its often blinkered defense of Second Amendment rights. Whether violent media does or does not influence player behavior, the NRA and Crave Entertainment's claim that *Gun Club* is a "nonviolent" game deals a fascinating counterpoint to the gunplay fantasy common to commercial games. Gun sport, it turns out, is a monotonous affair filled mostly with managing equipment and waiting. For those who find it pleasur-able, the pleasure lies largely in the mastery of mechanism. When the weapon's destructive power produces excitement, it's an ex-citement contextualized in reverence, even anxiety, accentuated by the relative rarity of actually firing a shot. And perhaps this is exactly the type of gun fantasy we really need.

NRA Gun Club's ability to present the detachment of gun use arises from its earnestness, an earnestness that doesn't come with-out considerable work. It's a rule that can be best shown through exception. Consider *Torture Game 2*, a simple web game in which players can inflict various bloody punishments (spikes, gunfire, razor, ropes, and more) on a rag doll, physics-driven character dangling from a rope.

In an MSNBC article critiquing the game, the journalist Winda Benedetti reports that the game's nineteen-year-old developer had seemingly little in mind when he created it.[4] For critics of games of this sort, it's tempting to conclude that the subject mat-ter causes the problem: a game about torture could never be a good idea. But as *NRA Gun Club* suggests, deliberateness and dryness might be the best way to simulate something horrifying. It's precisely the *lack* of earnestness and depth of simulation that makes *Torture Game 2* offensive, not its subject matter.

Torture is not the same as random violence. Torture is physi-cal or mental suffering conducted for punishment or compliance. The process of being tortured is traumatic precisely because death or madness is not immediately desired, but the fear and sensation of those conditions arise almost immediately. This game doesn't attempt to address the experience of the tortured, so I'll leave that interesting question aside for the moment. From the torturer's perspective, the attitude and resolve required to carry out the act itself is most worthy of understanding and dismissal. The grue-someness of *Torture Game 2* pales in comparison with the his-tory and present of real torture. Just compare the real devices of torture with the anonymous ones present in the game: the choke pear, a wood or iron device used to lock a victim's mouth open;

the heretic's fork, a bipronged sharpened fork placed between the chin and sternum used to prevent a victim from moving his head; the Judas chair, a sharpened wooden point used to stretch the orifices of a victim suspended above it; or waterboarding, the most recently reviled, a method meant to induce the feeling of drowning.

What's it like actually to enact torture? That's a topic a videogame offers a unique position to understand, by simulating the experience of its motivation, its enactment, and its consequence. What's the sensation of clamping down the head crusher one more turn as your victims scream in agony as their teeth first crack, then their eyes squeeze from their sockets, and finally, if desired, their very necks shatter? What's it like to pour buckets of water over a thrashing but silenced victim whose brain is tricked into the panic of suffocation? What's it like to hear but not heed the desperate cries for mercy in pursuit of information or confession? Or, on the other side of things, what's it like on the way to market to pass a man every day slowly dying of the gangrene infection wrought by the chair of torture, set there as an example.

But the doll in *Torture Game 2* does not cry, or wince, or respond in any way save for the physics of its inverse kinematics and the careful spatter of its blood. We're not forced to feel the tender burst of flesh as razor enters thigh, or the buttery passage of chainsaw through forearm. No social context motivates us or makes us pause with confusion, misgiving, or regret. *Torture Game 2* is a voodoo doll, not a torture simulator. It allows us to imagine we're inflicting suffering but without taking on the agency or consequence of the act itself.

Yet just as there are videogames like *NRA Gun Club* that make the common simulated act of gunfire seem boring or undesirable, so there are videogames that come closer to an earnest simulation of torture. The best one is *Manhunt* (where "best" means "most repugnant"). The game tells the story of a sociopath denied his own death (itself a kind of torture) in exchange for slavery as a mercenary butcher. The acts themselves are heinous, yet the game succeeds in making the player feel motivated to conduct them. One feels the dissonant reverberations of that pleasure long after playing.

When a sequel was released for the Nintendo Wii, it met a firestorm of controversy thanks to the addition of gestural interfaces to the game's demented acts: now you could "really" saw off a limb, garrote a neck, or grip and tear at a victim's testicles.[5] The context this time is pure psychosis, but the effects now become physical as well as visual. The player feels the same disgust and intrigue as in the original game, but now he or she must also reconcile a physiological response: the burn of muscle from virtual sawing, the racing heartbeat of exertion.

Much of the controversy surrounding *Manhunt 2* was directed precisely at the gestural controls of the Wii edition. Actually embodying these sadistic acts, many argued, edged too close to a murder simulator. But these critics get it precisely backward. A murder simulator *ought to revile us*, the more the better. If anything, trivializing death and torture through abstraction is far more troublesome than attenuating it through ghastly representation. *Torture Game 2* fails not because it makes us feel pleasure but because it makes us feel nothing, or not enough anyway, about the acts it allows us to perform. We should simulate torture not to take the place of real acts but to renew our disgust for them.

20 Drill

When considering the unique powers of videogames, we may cite their ability to engage us in thorny challenges, to envelop our attention and commitment, to overwhelm our senses and intellects as we strive to master physical trials of a battle or work out the optimal strategy for an economy.

Usually we're right when we think this, no matter the subject or purpose of the game. Indeed, one benefit of games over media like print, image, and film is how effectively they occupy our attention, forcing us to become practitioners of their problems rather than casual observers. From algebra to zombies, good games captivate us with sophistication of thought and action.

If we imagine that this sophistication is the gain on an amplifier, we might realize that some problems don't need the levels cranked up to eleven. And not just because they're casual games or games meant to relax us or to facilitate our interaction with friends. No, some games just don't take on topics that interesting. They're regimens more than experiences. Tools more than art. Drills more than challenges.

The International Civil Aviation Organization requires that flight crews provide passengers with explanations of the safety and emergency features of a commercial aircraft before takeoff. If you're a frequent flyer, you've heard such demonstrations enough that you probably ignore them. Air travel is very safe, after all, far safer than driving. According to statistics aggregated by the science news source LiveScience, the odds of dying in an airplane crash in the United States are 1 in 20,000, compared with 1 in 246 for falling down, 1 in 100 for motor vehicle accidents, and 1 in 5 for

< 141 >

heart disease.[1] Statistically, the flight safety demonstration would be more productively used to dissuade passengers from eating at the fast-food restaurants in the terminal on arrival.

Despite the low risk, who can't spare five minutes? Why not figure out where the nearest exits are and remind yourself how the oxygen masks work? The best reason is not the most obvious: the airlines' demonstration practices have actually made it harder to do so.

Things didn't used to be this way. As late as the midcentury, commercial air travel was downright dangerous. When boarding the luxurious Boeing B377 Stratocruiser in 1950, a Pan American passenger might have been well advised to study the safety card, given that thirteen of the fifty-six Stratocruisers built suffered hull-loss accidents between 1951 and 1970.

But today, as we jockey for overhead space and attempt to settle into the uncomfortable crush of economy class, air travel is too ordinary to merit curiosity, let alone fear. There are too many passengers and too little time to personalize. Thus the safety demonstration plays right into the weary ennui of contemporary air travel.

After September 11, flight attendants won a long-fought battle to be recognized as safety workers. The results have been helpful from a labor perspective, but they haven't done much for overall passenger safety. As Drew Whitelegg describes in his book about flight attendants, *Working the Skies*, airlines don't draw any more attention to matters of safety than they absolutely must, lest they turn off rather than attract customers.[2]

In some cases, like Southwest Airlines' famous safety rap, individual flight attendants have taken it on themselves to liven up the cabin, to make the announcements more fun (and probably to make their jobs more tolerable). More recently, the airlines have adopted a similar approach as an official corporate strategy. For example, my hometown airline Delta introduced a new safety video in 2008, featuring a shapely strawberry-blonde flight attendant as its narrator. The video included numerous cuts to close-crops of her face, accentuating her high cheekbones and full lips.

At one point, she playfully wags a finger in front of the camera, rejoining: "Smoking is *not allowed* on any Delta flight."

Her name is Katherine Lee, and she's actually a Delta flight attendant, not just a spokesmodel. The Internet dubbed her "Deltalina" thanks to her resemblance to sexpot actress Angelina Jolie (she's since adopted the name and become a minor celebrity). The YouTube video of her security shtick has been viewed over two million times.[3] She's appeared on television talk shows and on CNN. Wired.com called her "Delta's Sexy Safety Starlet."[4] In a weird historical inversion, this very much *is* your father's Pan Am.

In a similar, yet weirder maneuver, Air New Zealand ran an in-flight safety video with its cabin crew, both male and female, totally naked but emblazoned with body-paint uniforms. Careful framing and cuts ensure the video is totally PG (there's a blurry booty shot at the end), but the intention is clear: reinvigorate attention by giving passengers something they want to look at.

And these videos certainly have made passengers pay more attention, even if they've also perpetuated a retrograde picture of the air hostess as sex object. In the words of the Delta manager who produced the Deltalina video, they "make sure [our customers] know what to do in the event of an emergency . . . adding bits of humor and unexpected twists to something pretty standard."[5] Yet, in making the safety briefing more interesting, efforts like those of Delta and Air New Zealand actually *reduce* its ability to communicate safety information, if that was even possible.

Live safety demonstration raps or videos with bombshells hope to raise our interest above the level that a printed pamphlet, illustrated card, filmed demonstration, or live display can accomplish. The pique works; we hear and see them (Rapper Steward is funny, Katherine Lee is beautiful). But what we attend to is not the material being delivered but the manner by which it's delivered. I've flown hundreds of thousands of miles on Delta since Deltalina made her debut, but I still have no idea where to find my life vest ("Life vests are either between your seats, under your seats, or in a compartment under your armrest"). Never mind the eight steps required to don one properly. The result is safety theater. Airlines perform the appearance of safety to comply with regulations while imposing the lowest cognitive and emotional burden possible on the passenger so as to suppress fear and agitation.

As anyone who's traveled on an ocean cruise knows, all passengers are required to participate in a "muster drill" soon after embarkation. Even though ships sink even more rarely than planes crash, international law requires the crew to conduct an actual drill (not just a demo) in which passengers must don their lifejackets and report to their assigned lifeboat stations within a certain amount of time.

The lessons learned from this practice are banal, but startling. It's easy to put on a life vest, once you've done it. It's easy to find the right lifeboat station, once you know where to look. It's easy to find the fastest route to that station, once you've tread it. But the first time, all of these tasks are confusing.

Likewise, it's easy to fasten and unfasten your airplane seatbelt, because you've done it so many times. Thankfully, I've never had to put on one of those yellow oxygen masks that may fall "in the unlikely event that cabin pressure changes." But if they did, despite myself, I bet I wouldn't know exactly what to do. Never mind finding the exit doors that have inflatable rafts instead of slides, or divining the proper way to unlatch and extract an exit door.

For some time now, emergency personnel have been using live-action role-play and computer simulation to drill emergency preparedness scenarios. Indeed, first responder simulations for paramedics and firefighters are among the most active areas of serious games development. For example, Virtual Heroes has created *HumanSim,* a sophisticated medical simulation for health professionals to try out unusual scenarios, including responding to "rare conditions or events."

But these drills are complex and expensive, even if they're less complex and expensive when simulated instead of carried out on real city streets with real equipment. Indeed, cost-effectiveness is one reason serious games appeal to the organizations and municipalities that use them for this purpose.

DRILL   < 145 >

Drill in games has traditionally been understood as the digitization of skill exercises. *Math Blaster, Reader Rabbit,* and other edutainment titles are the obvious examples, with their chocolate-covered broccoli approach to arithmetic or phonics. The seat belt, the life vest, and the emergency exit represent a type of task simpler and less challenging than the emergency response scenario, yet a more complex, less boring sort than kiddie drill and skill. One doesn't really need to practice seat buckling and life vest donning very often. Once might be enough. But that one time sure is useful.

It's helpful to contrast *HumanSim* with the Deltalina video and the muster drill. The first uses sophisticated artificial intelligence to simulate the interrelated effects of split-second decisions. The next uses understated naughtiness to incrementally greater attention. And the last uses the nuisance of drill to get passengers to figure out how to put on a life vest. There's potential in this last kind of drill, the "do it once, know it well enough" sort. It's an application domain we deal with constantly: how would I get to the emergency exit? How do I operate my cruise control? How do I pick my child up from summer day camp?

Most of these tasks are simple ones. But they are still complex enough to recommend consideration as processes rather than as simple sets of instructions. It might be raining when it's time to fetch junior, or one of the nearest exits might be blocked with debris. This sort of drill doesn't just mean rote practice, as in *Math Blaster,* nor does it involve complex dynamics with unpredictable feedback loops and race conditions, as in *HumanSim.* And instead of doing whatever it is the task demands, we would simulate it.

Perhaps the best example of a game that does this sort of simulated drill is *Cooking Mama,* a series of kitchen simulation games. Mama helpfully guides the player through the steps involved in preparing a dish—filleting the fish, sautéing the seasonings, dressing the plate. And Mama chides and berates the player when he or she does it wrong. While I probably wouldn't want to eat a meal prepared by someone who had cooked only in *Cooking Mama,* I would feel oddly more confident in such a chef's ability in the kitchen than in the case of someone who had only ever watched Rachael Ray.

Cooking Mama aspires for more aesthetic ends, goals beyond a simple tool. But as a conceptual model, it offers a good starting example of a drill game. One closer to the spirit of a real drill is Drivers Ed Direct's *Parallel Parking Game.* It does just what the title says: the player parallel parks a car, trying to avoid collisions. Sure, the keyboard controls are unlike those of a real car and the game's physics are unrealistic, but the drill approach is very much present: by trying the task in the game, one gets a preliminary sense of what it involves, how to approach success, and how to avoid failure.

There aren't many games like this, but there could be. Think of all the other things you'd benefit from trying out once before having to do them in earnest: changing a diaper, threading a needle, negotiating a car purchase, loading a dishwasher, carving a turkey, waxing a sports car, ironing a shirt, wrapping a gift, tasting a wine, assembling a bookshelf, staging a pickup, scolding a child, recording a television program. None of these are terribly monumental or interesting acts; indeed many are about as banal as it gets. But almost anything is challenging once.

Consider the commercial airliner once more. Every seat on every flight I take has a personal video display on which I watch Katherine Lee wag her finger and pout her lips at me. Each screen is also a terminal running a little Linux distribution, and I can already play trivia and blackjack and *Zuma* on it. It even knows the location of my seat and, presumably, the type of aircraft that's about to hurtle me across the ocean at five hundred miles per hour. What if I could choose to run a little practice drill, following those white emergency lights amid the darkness and smoke and chaos, to one of those eight emergency exits, whose door I might have to shimmy open and whose raft I might have to deploy, in order that I might defy those 1 in 20,000 odds and survive. Wouldn't that be a better use of a few minutes of my life than lusting after Katherine Lee?

The End of Gamers

We like to think that technological progress is spectacular. Whether our attitudes follow Clay Shirky's celebration or Nicholas Carr's censure, we remain certain that something dramatic will happen. Either new computer technologies will help solve our most pressing problems, or they'll create even more pressing problems demanding totally different solutions. No matter the case, one thing is sure: the present is sensational, and the future will only be more so.

Certainly it's true that media do sometimes dramatically change the way we live. The internetworked digital computer may be poised to join media like toolmaking, agriculture, metallurgy, the alphabet, the chariot, the printing press, and alternating current as forces that have altered the shape of human life and experience fundamentally and forever. But within the wake of media ecologies like these, smaller ebbs and flows make increasingly smaller waves. They just make more of them. Within an ecology, the individual actions of particular creatures exert local forces on the overall system. Media microecology steps in here, asking modest, pragmatic, but still consequential questions about the internal operation of particular media microhabitats.

In this book I've tried to dig in the dirt of videogames' media ecosystem. I've not set out to present a complete inventory of all the ways videogames are put to use, but to offer a variety of examples that demonstrate their rich variety and complexity. I've tried to show that much has already been done with games, even if many more applications have not been explored fully. Still others have yet to be discovered, and perhaps you may be inspired to

< 147 >

stake out your own tiny corner of videogame earth and see what strange playable creatures might thrive there.

But we must face a humbling and perhaps even disturbing conclusion about the media forms we love: they're just not that special. Indeed, they become less special by the day, as they do more for us and as we discover more about them. We don't need more media ecologists raising their fists in boosterism or detraction, painting overly general pictures with broad brushes. We need more media entomologists and media archaeologists overturning rocks and logs to find and explain the tiny treasures that would otherwise go unseen. We need more media particle physicists and media nanotechnologists explaining the strange interactions of the tiniest examples of various media, videogames among them.

When it comes to a spread of access and use in media, we often hear growth celebrated as "democratization." As tools and distribution channels become cheaper and more accessible, their spoils are thought to be available to everyone rather than just to some well-trained, highly capitalized creative elite. But such access comes at a price: the loss of scarcity, of novelty, of curiosity, of surprise. Walter Benjamin recognized that mechanically reproduced works of art lose their ritual value, their "aura," but he also predicted that such media (particularly film) would enjoy new adoption in politics as a result.[1] Benjamin was right to some extent, but his prediction was too narrow. As it turns out, mechanically reproducible media can be put to myriad uses, from crass advertising to high art to political intervention to new ritual practices. It's not the aura that declines in the maturity of a medium but its character, its wildness. Media are not democratized; they're tamed instead.

Journalists, pundits, and professors are unlikely to come to such a conclusion, partly because they rely on novelty, curiosity, and drama to make compelling claims worthy of big headlines, large book contract advances, or incendiary provocations. For this reason, we might want to look to other sorts of folk for new media strategies.

Who would serve as a less traditional media theorist than the fashion mogul Marc Ecko? His eponymous clothing company brings in $1.5 billion a year in revenue.[2] While he's best known for rhino-emblazoned T-shirts, shoes, and underpants, Ecko has branched out to popular media in recent years, starting up the consumer culture rag *Complex Magazine,* the extreme lifestyle YouTube knock-off eckotv.com, and the videogame *Mark Ecko's Getting Up: Contents under Pressure.* On his corporate website, Ecko cites attention deficit disorder as an inspiration that he's built his world around.[3]

After the release of his videogame, a canned interview with Ecko ran in popular magazines like *Wired,* paid for by the financial consultants CIT Group. It's one of those "special advertising sections" designed to integrate so seamlessly into the magazine that it's easy to mistake it for editorial content. In the interview, Ecko explains "what's next" for his growing conglomerate:

> I want to keep growing in the video-gaming space. I believe it's the Wild West of media culture. There's something magical and abstract about gaming. Games aren't yet demystified—versus movies, for example; there are TV shows about the making of movies.[4]

Ecko's point is both insightful and ironic. It contains a complex observation about the current state of videogames as a medium. Television is so familiar, it's not even startling to think about TV programming produced solely to discuss other media forms. The same could not even be imagined for videogames. The form in which the insight is presented only reiterates Ecko's point: his comments appear as a paid advertisement simulating a magazine interview, an absurd situation that's nevertheless completely legible to the millions of magazine readers whose eyes pass over it. Magazines and television are just too mundane, too boring for these things to be very surprising.

Ecko is not interested in the mundane; his sights are firmly set on the flashier side of the medium he already began to explore in *Getting Up,* itself a critically underappreciated game that hides a critique of an autocratic police state in a game about graffiti.[5] But we can turn his observation on its head and use it to set a compass bearing for the future of videogames: *demystification.*

One way to make games more ordinary and familiar is to help them realize their place in meaningful art and culture. Indeed, that's the primary strategy one finds in the commercial game industry. Whether successful or not, the industry strives for Hollywood blockbuster–style spectacles. The fledgling indie game scene often privileges new gameplay mechanics or subjects for games, but just as frequently it showcases the hopeful yet derivative swing of so many minor leaguers trying to break into the majors. Despite major differences, both efforts trace the earnest hope that videogames are an expressive medium as important and viable as film or literature, but different in form. It's a fine goal.

But as videogames become more familiar, they also become less edgy and exciting. This is what Ecko means when he talks about demystification. Over time, media become domesticated, and domestication is a mixed blessing. On the one hand, it allows broader reach and scale. It means that more people can understand and manipulate a medium. Grandma and grandpa understand what it means to watch a VHS tape or a DVD of junior's birthday or karate tournament; television viewers see beyond the sheen of an advertisement to learn about the product it peddles; a couple settles in to watch a movie downloaded from Netflix on a Friday night. On the other hand, it makes a once exotic, wild medium tame and uninteresting.

Indeed, gamers already find themselves disturbed and disoriented at the domestication of what was once a private, dangerous wilderness. Social games played on Facebook offer one frontier that's been overrun with unwelcome settlers in the minds of many computer and console game players. As the social game designer Tami Baribeau explains, traditional gamers hate games like *FarmVille*: "Compared to traditional games, Facebook games are simplistic, almost childish in art style, relatively shallow, not too difficult to master, and not 'cool' to play or talk about."[6] Yet, as Baribeau reminds us in their defense, tens of millions of people play these games. Numbers alone don't make *FarmVille* safe from accusations of bad art or corrupt manipulation (I've made these accusations myself, in fact).[7] But nevertheless, these games exist, whether or not we like them. And more of them are coming, hacking through the brush with their machetes, plotting out future homesteads.

Domestication is violent and tragic. It strips the stallion of some of its power and magic and beauty. But it also allows the cow to be ranched and milked, and the dog to herd the sheep, and the wheat to be predictably germinated. Some species of videogame will always remain wild, like the warthog or the kudzu. But they'll be the exceptions.

If we think of the possibility space for games as a more complex, graduated space, in which many kinds of experiences could be touched by games, then many more kinds of innovation present themselves. But more so, the more such opportunities game makers and players exploit, the more deeply videogames become familiar, and the more rapidly at that. Such a perspective forces us to *hope* games will be more ordinary, more mundane. Not just some games: we should want many of them, maybe even *most* of them, to be ordinary and familiar, their particular purpose a footnote rather than a billboard.

Consider an example. In 2005 my game studio Persuasive Games created *Stone City*, a training game for the Cold Stone Creamery ice cream franchise. In the game, the player services customers at the popular mix-your-own-flavor ice cream franchise by assembling the proper concoctions while allocating generally profitable portion sizes. Since its release, we've received frequent phone calls and emails from the general public, expressing interest in playing the game. The vast majority of people who contact us are not human resources managers or training executives looking to build their own corporate games. They're ordinary people who are simply curious about it.

You'd never expect such interest if you read Justin Peters's *Slate* riposte to educational games. As Peters charges of our game, "Animating mindless, boring repetition doesn't make the repetition any less mindless or boring. No sane Cold Stone employee will be fooled into thinking that *Stone City* is anything other than a soul-crushing training exercise."[8] Why, then, would so many ordinary people go out of their way to express interest? Perhaps some aren't clear that the game was commissioned as a training tool and not a leisure game. Perhaps some are misinformed teenagers yet to be disillusioned by a soul-crushing job. Perhaps others are as smart and skeptical as Peters suspects they might be, and they want to see how possible workplaces represent their expectations for labor.

But I bet most of them just like ice cream. They find intrigue in the Cold Stone method of service, which involves bashing together flavors and toppings on a frozen granite slab. They want to have a go at it for a few minutes.

Peters's ideal model for educational games is *Civilization*, Sid Meier's classic game about building a society based on scarcity of resources. There's no doubt that *Civ* is a great game, one that any designer could learn from no matter his or her expressive goals. And Peters is right that there's considerable educational potential in this kind of game; Kurt Squire, an education scholar, even made it the topic of his doctoral dissertation.[9] But *Civilization* is just one kind of game. It's a kind of game that demands significant commitment and devotion. It's a gamer's kind of game.

Are the would-be players of *Stone City* just too stupid or inexperienced to know about the much more complex and sophisticated kinds of games that they could get their hands on instead? I don't think so. I bet many of them have even played *Civ*. I think they're looking for a different kind of experience, one that might not have as much to do with videogames as it does with ice cream shops. *Stone City* serves at least two purposes, then: one to educate line workers in the frozen dessert industry, and another just to satisfy the curiosity of people for whom ice cream satisfies a sweet tooth. It, along with all the other examples discussed in this book, offers a tiny taste of the mundane future of videogames.

Instead of chasing after a mythical videogame *Citizen Kane* or trying to reconcile all videogames with one monolithic set of laws for design and reception, what if we followed Ecko's provocation to demystify games. What if we allowed that videogames have many possible goals and purposes, each of which couples with many possible aesthetics and designs to create many possible player experiences, none of which bears any necessary relationship to the commercial videogame industry as we currently know it. The more things games can do, the more the general public will become accepting of, and interested in, the medium in general.

A summary of that future would have no place on a T-shirt or poster. It wouldn't be worth quoting as a sound bite on television or splashed across the cover of a nonfiction bestseller. It would state the obvious, with humility: videogames can do many things. They do so every day, whether or not people notice them. They do so in public and in private. They do so with and without fanfare. Counterintuitive though it may be, that's a future in which videogames win their battle in the culture wars and become relevant and lasting.

For decades, videogames have been played primarily by the people who already play videogames and who consider the playing of videogames a part of their identity. But other sorts of people abound: people who fly for business more than three times a month, people who read all of the Sunday newspaper, or people who have kids with food allergies. I am sure these people read magazines and watch television and listen to the radio, but no right-minded person would label them *ziners* or *tubers* or *airwavers*. They're just people, with interests, who sometimes consume different kinds of media as they go about their lives.

If videogame playership is indeed broadening, then videogames will no longer fall under the sole purview of the games industry. There'll no longer be a single court in which the legiti-macy of games will be tried. There'll no longer be an oligarchy of videogame industrialist-gods to whom all creators and players will pay homage. Instead, there'll be many smaller groups, com-munities, and individuals with a wide variety of interests, some of them occasionally intersecting with particular videogame titles.

Some might argue that as videogames broaden in appeal, players' demands will only increase. Games will have to become more and more gamey, more like commercial videogames of the current industrial variety to meet the increasingly sophisticated demands of these new players as more and more of them become gamers. But I suggest the opposite: as videogames broaden in ap-peal, being a "gamer" will actually become less common, if being a gamer means consuming games as one's primary media diet or identifying with videogames as a primary part of one's identity. The demands of players will surely increase and deepen, but those demands may bear little resemblance to the ones gamers place on games today.

Soon gamers will be the anomaly. If we're very fortunate, they'll disappear altogether. Instead we'll just find people, ordi-nary people of all sorts. And sometimes those people will play videogames. And it won't be a big deal, at all.

Notes

Introduction

1. Nicholas Carr, *The Shallows: What the Internet Is Doing to Our Brains* (New York: Norton, 2010), 10.

2. Clay Shirky, *Cognitive Surplus: Creativity and Generosity in a Connected Age* (New York: Penguin, 2010), 37.

3. Matthew Battles, "Reading Isn't Just a Monkish Pursuit," Nieman Journalism Lab, June 29, 2010, http://www.niemanlab.org/2010/06/reading-isnt-just-a-monkish-pursuit-matthew-battles-on-the-shallows/.

4. Marshall McLuhan, *The Gutenberg Galaxy: The Making of Typographic Man* (Toronto: University of Toronto Press, 1962), 120–26.

5. Marshall McLuhan, *Understanding Media: The Extensions of Man* (New York: McGraw Hill, 1964), 7.

6. Ibid., 24, 26.

7. For more about serious games, see http://www.seriousgames.org. My approach to such games, which I term *persuasive games* rather than serious games, can be found in Ian Bogost, *Persuasive Games: The Expressive Power of Videogames* (Cambridge, Mass.: MIT Press, 2007).

8. Marshall McLuhan, *Understanding Me: Lectures and Interviews,* edited by Stephanie McLuhan and David Staines (Cambridge, Mass.: MIT Press, 2004), 271.

9. Neil Postman, *Technopoly: The Surrender of Culture to Technology* (New York: Vintage, 1993), 18.

1. Art

1. Roger Ebert, "Answer Man," *Chicago Sun-Times,* November 27, 2005, http:// rogerebert.suntimes.com/apps/pbcs.dll/section?category=ANSWERMAN&date=20051127. The history of Ebert's

< 155 >

public statements about videogames is complex, mostly because they developed originally in a series of offhanded comments in various articles, which later developed into more formal writings. The best account of the early stages of the debate comes from the Indy Gamer blog (http://indygamer.blogspot.com/2007/07/debate-arthouse-games-vs-ebert.html), which explains that Ebert's first formal position on games (cited above) came from a reader letter responding to his October 21, 2005, review of the film adaptation of *Doom* (http://rogerebert.suntimes.com/apps/pbcs.dll/article?AID=/20051020/REVIEWS/51012003/1023).

2. Jim Preston, "The Arty Party," *Gamasutra*, February 11, 2008, http:// www.gamasutra.com/view/feature/3536/the_arty_party.php.

3. Roger Ebert, "Games vs. Art: Ebert vs. Barker," *Chicago Sun-Times*, July 21, 2007, http://rogerebert.suntimes.com/apps/pbcs.dll/article?AID=/20070721/COMMENTARY/70721001.

4. See http://www.medienkunstnetz.de/works/super-mario-cloud/.

5. In a move he calls "an admission of failure," Humble has written an extensive statement about *The Marriage*, which includes a complete description of its rules and his interpretation of their meaning. It can be found at http:// www.rodvik.com/rodgames/marriage.html.

6. Bogost, *Persuasive Games*, 28–29.

7. Janet Murray, *Hamlet on the Holodeck: The Future of Narrative in Cyberspace* (Cambridge, Mass.: MIT Press, 1997), 144.

8. Auriea Harvey and Michaël Samyn, "Realtime Art Manifesto," paper presented at the Seventh Annual Mediaterra Festival of Art and Technology, Athens, Greece, October 4–8, 2006, http://www.tale-of-tales.com/tales/RAM.html.

2. Empathy

1. Little evidence exists to confirm the exact sum, but historical reports usually fall between $20 and $25 million. See Matt Barton and Bill Loguidice, "A History of Gaming Platforms: Atari 2600 Video Computer System/VCS," *Gamasutra*, February 28, 2008, http:// www.gamasutra.com/view/feature/3551/a_history_of_gaming_platforms_.php. Whatever the exact licensing fee was, it was clearly sizable.

2. This too is an apocryphal story; however, it appears to be true. For more, see Nick Montfort and Ian Bogost, *Racing the Beam: The Atari Video Computer System* (Cambridge, Mass.: MIT Press, 2009), 127.

3. Sandra Cisneros, *The House on Mango Street* (New York: Vintage, 1991).

4. *Short Cuts,* directed by Robert Altman (Los Angeles: Fine Line Features, 1993).

3. Reverence

1. "Sony Apologises over Violent Game," *BBC News,* June 15, 2007, http://news.bbc.co.uk/2/hi/uk_news/england/manchester/6758381.stm.

2. "Cathedral row over video war game," *BBN News,* June 9, 2007, http://news.bbc.co.uk/2/hi/uk_news/england/manchester/6736809.stm.

3. Ibid.

4. Ibid.

4. Music

1. Murad Ahmed, "Guitar Hero Leads Children to Pick Up Real Instruments," *The Times* (London), December 1, 2008, http:// technology.timesonline.co.uk/tol/news/tech_and_web/gadgets_and_gaming/article5266959.ece.

2. John Sharp, Jesper Juul, Frank Lantz, and Christoph Kluetsch, Panel Discussion at the Art History of Games Symposium, Woodruff Center for the Arts, Atlanta, Georgia, February 5, 2010.

3. Slavoj Žižek, *The Parallax View* (Cambridge, Mass.: MIT Press, 2006), 3.

5. Pranks

1. Ricky Gervais, *The Office* (London: BBC, 2001–2003).

2. For more on Robinett's hidden message, see Montfort and Bogost, *Racing the Beam,* 59–61.

3. Ibid., 61.

4. See http://www.rtmark.com/simcopter.html.

5. Adam Steinbaugh, "The SimCopter Scandal: An Interview with Jacques Servin," SimEden.com, http:// www.rtmark.com/more/articles/simedensimcopterinterview.html [archived].

6. Madeleine Smithberg and Lizz Winstead, *The Daily Show* (New York: Comedy Central, 1996–).

6. Transit

1. Wolfgang Schivelbusch, *The Railway Journey: The Industrialization of Time and Space in the 19th Century* (Berkeley: University of California Press, 1977), 7.

2. Ibid., 37–38.

3. Walter Benjamin, "The Work of Art in the Age of Mechanical Reproduction," *Illuminations: Essays and Reflections,* edited by Hannah Arendt and translated by Harry Zohn (New York: Schocken, 1969), 221–26.

4. Schivelbusch, *Railway Journey,* 36.

5. Ibid., 24.

6. Ibid., 64.

7. Ibid., 62.

7. Branding

1. The new properties were decided by popular vote of the general public; according to Hasbro, over three million online votes were tallied.

2. Philip Orbanes, *Monopoly: The World's Most Famous Game and How It Got That Way* (New York: Da Capo, 2006), 33–34.

3. Stuart Elliott, "Would You Like Fries with That Monopoly Game?," *New York Times,* September 12, 2006, http:// www.nytimes.com/2006/09/12/business/media/12adco.html.

4. Ibid.

5. Bogost, *Persuasive Games,* 199.

6. I've suggested the term *anti-advergames* for this type of social critique. See Bogost, *Persuasive Games,* 223.

7. Kevin Roberts, *Lovemarks: The Future beyond Brands* (New

York: Power House Books, 2005). For a collection of lovemarks, visit Robert's companion website at http:// www.lovemarks.com.

8. Some $750 million in total. See http://www.opensecrets.org/pres08/summary.php?id=n00009638.

9. Devlin Barrett, "Ads for Obama Campaign: 'It's in the Game,'" *Associated Press,* October 14, 2008, http://www.msnbc.msn.com/id/27184857/.

10. David Kestenbaum, "The Digital Divide between McCain and Obama," *NPR's All Things Considered,* August 1, 2008, http://www.npr.org/templates/story/story.php?storyId=93185393.

8. Electioneering

1. Tom Loftus, "Skip the Speech and Play the Policy: New Political Games Aim to Persuade, Not Just Entertain," *MSNBC,* October 18, 2004, http://www.msnbc.msn.com/id/6256146/.

2. "Barack Obama's Remarks on Victory in Wisconsin Primary," *Washington Post,* February 19, 2008, http://www.washingtonpost.com/wp-dyn/content/article/2008/02/19/AR2008021903257.html.

9. Promotion

1. Stephen Totilo, "Burger King Video Games: Savvy or Creepy?," *MTV News,* December 14, 2006, http:// www.mtv.com/news/articles/1548023/20061214/story.jhtml.

2. *Akeelah and the Bee,* directed by Doug Atkinson (Santa Monica, CA: Lion's Gate, 2006).

3. See http://www.unlockxbox.com.

4. It didn't hurt that the promotion took place before the Xbox Live Arcade service was still finding its feet at the time. In 2006 the service was mostly releasing coin-op reissues rather than the new, original titles for which it is known today.

5. Reuters, "Xbox Promotion, Value Menu Lift Burger King Earnings," *USA Today,* January 30, 2007, http:// www.usatoday.com/money/companies/earnings/2007-01-30-burgerking_x.htm.

6. Bogost, *Persuasive Games,* 199–223.

10. Snapshots

1. Sims Carnival and Popfly closed their doors their doors entirely, while Metaplace and Playcrafter changed the focus of their businesses from user creation to Facebook games. As with other "user-generated content" companies, these and other start-ups hoped to build a user-base significant enough to generate revenue or, more likely, to attract an acquisition from a larger company. Such was the case for Metaplace, which was acquired by Playdom in mid-2010.

2. Find each of these tools at http:// www.yoyogames.com/ gamemaker, http://www.adventuregamestudio.co.uk, and http:// www.rpgmaker.net, respectively.

11. Texture

1. Tom Bramwell, " 'Non-sexual' Rez trance vibrator was my idea—Mizuguchi," *Eurogamer,* July 25, 2006, http:// www.eurogamer. net/article.php?article_id=66297; Jane Pinkard, "Sex in Games: Rez+Vibrator," *Game Girl Advance,* October 26, 2002, http:// www.gamegirladvance.com/archives/2002/10/26/sex_in_games_ rezvibrator.html.

12. Kitsch

1. 60 Minutes, "Thomas Kinkade: A Success," *CBS News,* July 4, 2004, http:// www.cbsnews.com/stories/2001/11/21/60minutes/ main318790.shtml.

2. Max Horkheimer and Theodor Adorno, *The Dialectic of Enlightenment,* trans. Edmund Jephcott (Stanford, Calif.: Stanford University Press, 2002), 108–14.

13. Relaxation

1. Irene Chien, "This Is Not a Dance," *Film Quarterly* 59, no. 3 (2006): 22–34.

2. http:// www.jenovachen.com/flowingames/cloud.htm.

3. See Mihaly Csikszentmihalyi, *Flow: The Psychology of Optimal Experience* (New York: Harper and Row, 1990).

4. As PopCap stated in a press release announcing the avail-
ability of *Chuzzle*. For the full text, see http://www.gamestooge.
com/2007/05/29/popcap-brings-chuzzle-to-mobiles/.

5. Celia Pearce, "Sims, BattleBots, Cellular Automata God, and
Go," *Game Studies* 2, no. 1 (2002), http://www.gamestudies.org/0102/
pearce/.

6. Desert Bus is probably most well-known for its role in the annual
Child's Play charity event. Players accept pledges for time spent driving
in the game, the proceeds of which go to donations for toys and games
for hospital-bound kids. See http:// desertbus.org and http://www.
childsplaycharity.org for more.

14. Throwaways

1. See http://www.igda.org/wiki/Casual_Games_SIG.

2. Scott Cohen, *Zap! The Rise and Fall of Atari* (New York: McGraw-
Hill, 1983), 70–75.

3. As of August 2010, the average price of an iPhone game was $1.24.
See Richard Meads, "$1.24 the Average Price for iPhone Games," *Pocket
Gamer,* August 31, 2010, http:// www.pocketgamer.co.uk/r/iPhone/
App+Store/news.asp?c=23163.

4. Ian Bogost, Simon Ferrari, and Bobby Schweizer, *Newsgames:
Journalism at Play* (Cambridge, Mass.: MIT Press, 2010), 6, 11–34.

5. Ibid.

15. Titillation

1. Steve Lohr, "In Video Game, a Download Unlocks Hidden
Sex Scenes," *New York Times,* July 11, 2005, http://www.nytimes.
com/2005/07/11/technology/11game.html.

2. Joel Johnson, "Lesbian Alien Sex Scene from *Mass Effect*
Game," *Boing Boing,* November 12, 2007, http://gadgets.boingboing.
net/2007/11/12/lesbian-alien-sex-sc.html.

3. The most egregiously biased example aired on Fox News, in
a conversation between the host Martha MacCallum, the SpikeTV
host/critic Geoff Keighley, and Cooper Lawrence. The exchange,
which took place in January 2008, is summarized and transcribed on

the game journalism site Game Politics: http:// www.gamepolitics. com/2008/01/22/1993.

4. Even Apple's far more varied App Store content has an established record of refusing to publish products with sexual content or of removing them after publication. See Dan Frommer, "Apple Boots Sex Apps from iPhone App Store after Our Bombshell Exposé," *Business Insider*, February 19, 2010, http:// www.businessinsider.com/ apple-boots-some-sex-apps-from-iphone-app-store-2010-2.

5. Frank Lombardi, "Christine Quinn Rips 'Horrifying' Rape Game Rapelay," *New York Daily News*, February 24, 2009, http:// www. nydailynews.com/news/2009/02/23/2009-02-23_christine_quinn_ rips_horrifying_rape_gam.html.

6. Leigh Alexander, "And You Thought Grand Theft Auto Was Bad: Should the United States Ban a Japanese 'Rape Simulator' Game?," *Slate*, March 9, 2009, http://www.slate.com/id/2213073/pagenum/all/.

16. Exercise

1. For example, see Johanna Höysniemi, "Design and Evaluation of Physically Interactive Games" (PhD diss., Tampere University, 2006), http://acta.uta.fi/pdf/951-44-6694-2.pdf, or Debra Lieberman's ongoing work on the topic (http://www.comm.ucsb.edu/faculty/lieberman/ exergames.htm).

2. See http://wiinintendo.net/2006/12/05/wii-sports-experiment/.

3. From the product description at http://www.pixelmood.com/ arukotch.htm.

4. The official Nike+ website can be found at http://www.nike.com/ nikeplus/.

17. Work

1. Johan Huizinga, *Homo Ludens: A Study of the Play-Element in Culture* (New York: Routledge, 1949), 10.

2. J. L. Austin, "Performative-Constative," in *The Philosophy of Language*, ed. John Searle (Oxford: Oxford University Press, 1971), 13–22.

3. J. L. Austin, *How to Do Things with Words* (Cambridge, Mass.: Harvard University Press, 1975), 14, 42–45.

4. "Neuzeitliches Duellierungs Artefakt," or a "modern dueling artifact." From a promotional brochure, see http:// www.khm.de/~morawe/painstation/PainStation_ger.pdf.

5. The games are aggregated at http://gwap.com.

6. See http://images.google.com/imagelabeler.

18. Habituation

1. Philip E. Orbanes, *The Game Makers: The Story of Parker Brothers, from Tiddledy Winks to Trivial Pursuit* (Cambridge, Mass.: Harvard Business School Press, 2003), 13. I am grateful to Jesper Juul for bringing this passage to my attention.

2. Tracy Fullerton, "GDC Microtalks," session at the 2009 Game Developers Conference, San Francisco, March 26, 2009.

3. Orbanes, *Game Makers*, 13.

4. *New York Times*, "Decline of Racquets as an Indoor Sport," January 4, 1906. Thanks again to Jesper Juul for bringing this example to my attention.

5. K. Thor Jensen, "The Truth about the Biz of Casual Games," *GigaOm*, May 2, 1998, http:// gigaom.com/2008/05/02/casual-games-the-bottom-line/.

6. Cf. David J.M. Kramer et al., "Musical Imagery: Sound of Silence Activates Auditory Cortex," *Nature*, March 10, 2005.

7. Joe Anuta, "What Makes a Song Catchy," *Research Penn State*, June 5, 2006, http://www.rps.psu.edu/probing/tunes.html.

19. Disinterest

1. Noah Wardrip-Fruin, "Two E3 Fantasies," *Grand Text Auto*, September 7, 2006, http://grandtextauto.org/2006/09/07/two-e3-fantasies/.

2. "*NRA Varmint Hunter* Reviews," *GameSpot*, February 8, 2006, http://www.gamespot.com/pc/sports/nravarminthunter/players.html?tag=tabs%3Breviews.

3. Jeff Gertsman, "*NRA Gun Club* Review," *GameSpot,* December 5, 2006, http://www.gamespot.com/ps2/action/gunclub/review. html?tag=tabs%3Breviews.

4. Winda Benedetti, "Should You Take 'Torture' Seriously?," *MSNBC,* June 24, 2008, http://www.msnbc.msn.com/id/25337373/ wid/11915829?GT1=40006.

5. Chris Kohler, "*Manhunt 2* Meltdown Shows Game-Killing Power of Adults-Only Rating," *Wired News,* August 22, 2007, http:// www. wired.com/gaming/gamingreviews/news/2007/08/esrb.

20. Drill

1. Robert Roy Britt, "The Odds of Dying," *LiveScience,* January 6, 2005, http:// www.livescience.com/environment/050106_odds_of_ dying.html.

2. Drew Whitelegg, *Working the Skies: The Fast-Paced, Disorienting World of the Flight Attendant* (New York: New York University Press, 2007), 110–16.

3. As of November 2010.

4. Joe Brown, "Delta's New Sexy Safety Starlet," *Wired,* March 26, 2008, http:// www.wired.com/autopia/2008/03/deltas-new-safe/.

5. Associated Press, "Safety Video Stars Delta Employee," *Yahoo News,* March 24, 2008, http:// news.yahoo.com/s/ ap_travel/20080324/ap_tr_ge/travel_brief_delta_video.

Conclusion

1. Walter Benjamin, "The Work of Art in the Age of Mechanical Reproduction," *Illuminations: Essays and Reflections,* edited by Hannah Arendt and translated by Harry Zohn (New York: Schocken, 1969), 230–45.

2. Arthur Lubow, " 'It's Going to Be Big,' " *Inc. Magazine,* March 1, 2009, http:// www.inc.com/magazine/20090301/its-going-to-be-big. html.

3. See http://www.marceckoenterprises.com/our-brands/.

4. *Wired,* May 2007, 41–44.

5. See Stephen Totilo's review of the game on MTV News: http://www.mtv.com/news/articles/1504962/20050629/index.jhtml.

6. Tami Baribeau, "Why Do Traditional Gamers Dislike Farmville?" *Examiner,* March 23, 2010, http://www.examiner.com/facebook-games-in-national/why-do-traditional-gamers-dislike-farmville. Baribeau herself does not share this opinion and expressed it in the introduction to her own riposte of social game critics.

7. My send-up of *FarmVille* and its ilk, titled *Cow Clicker,* can be played at http:// apps.facebook.com/cowclicker. For my explanation of that game, which includes my critique of the social game genre circa mid-2010, see Ian Bogost, "*Cow Clicker*: The Making of Obsession," *bogost.com,* July 21, 2010, http://www.bogost.com/blog/cow_clicker_1.shtml, and Leigh Alexander, "Interview: *Cow Clicker* Yields Ruminations on Social Gaming's Tense Battle Lines," *Gamasutra,* July 30, 2010, http://www.gamasutra.com/view/news/29618/Interview_Cow_Clicker_Yields_Ruminations_On_Social_Gamings_Tense_Battle_Lines.php.

8. Justin Peters, "World of Borecraft: Never Play a Videogame That's Trying to Teach You Something," *Slate,* June 27, 2007, http:// www.slate.com/id/2169019.

9. Kurt Squire, "Replaying History: Learning World History through Playing Civilization III" (PhD diss., Indiana University, 2004), http://website.education.wisc.edu/kdsquire/tenure-files/dissertation.html.

Gameography

Games discussed in the text are listed here, in alphabetical order by title. For more information about particular games, consult the archive at MobyGames.com or look for the titles by name at Wikipedia. Web addresses are provided here for games that can be played on or downloaded online.

Advance Wars. Game Boy Advance. Developed by Intelligent Systems Co. Nintendo, 2001.

Adventure. Atari Video Computer System (2600). Developed by Warren Robinett. Atari, 1978.

Airport Mania: First Flight. Windows, Mac, iPhone (2009). Developed by South Winds Games. Reflexive Entertainment, 2008.

America's Army: Operations. Linux, Macintosh, Windows. Developed and published by the U.S. Army, 2002. Updates and new versions were released for PC and console through 2009.

Animal Crossing. GameCube. Developed by Nintendo EAD. Nintendo, 2001. Other versions have appeared on Nintendo DS and Nintendo Wii.

Apple Season. Browser. Developed by Ferry Halim. Orisinal.com, undated. Available at http://www.ferryhalim.com/orisinal/g2/applegame.htm.

Asteroids. Coin-op. Developed by Lyle Rains and Ed Logg. Atari, 1979. Ported and adapted to numerous computers and consoles.

Attent. Windows/Microsoft Outlook. Developed and published by Seriosity, Inc., 2007. More information can be found at http://www.seriosity.com/products.html.

< 167 >

Bachelorette Party. Atari Video Computer System (2600). Developed and published by Mystique, 1982.

Beat 'Em & Eat 'Em. Atari Video Computer System (2600). Developed and published by Mystique, 1982.

Bejeweled. Browser, J2ME (mobile), Macintosh, PalmOS, Windows, Windows Mobile. Developed and published by PopCap, 2000. Numerous versions, sequels, and adaptations have appeared since, on many platforms.

Big Bumpin'. Xbox, Xbox 360. Developed by Blitz Arcade. King Games, 2006.

Bioshock. Macintosh, PlayStation 3, Windows, Xbox 360. Developed by 2K Boston and 2K Australia. 2K Games, 2007.

Braid. Xbox 360. Developed by Number None. Published by Microsoft Game Studios, 2008. Later released for Macintosh, PlayStation 3, and Windows.

Breakout. Coin-op. Developed and published by Atari, 1976. Ported and adapted to numerous computers and consoles.

Burning Desire/Jungle Fever. Atari Video Computer System (2600). Published by Playaround, circa 1983. Republished from rights purchased from the defunct Mystique.

Burnout: Paradise. PlayStation 3, Xbox 360, Windows. Developed by Criterion Studios. Electronic Arts, 2008.

Call of Duty. Macintosh, PlayStation, Windows, Xbox. Developed by Infinity Ward. Activision, 2003. Many sequels have appeared for numerous platforms.

Campaign Rush. Browser. Developed by Persuasive Games. CNN International, 2008. Available at http://edition.cnn.com/ELECTION/2008/campaign.rush.

Cathouse Blues/Gigolo. Atari Video Computer System (2600). Published by Playaround, circa 1983. Republished from rights purchased from the defunct Mystique.

Chuzzle. Mobile (many platforms). Developed by Raptisoft. PopCap Games, 2005.

City of Wonder. Web/Facebook. Developed and published by Playdom, 2010. Available at http://www.facebook.com/cityofwonder.

Cloud. Windows. Developed by students at the Division of Interactive Media at the University of Southern California School of Cinema and Television, 2005. Available at http://interactive.usc.edu/projects/cloud.

Colossal Cave. PDP-10. Developed by William Crowther and Don Woods. Ported and adapted to numerous minicomputer and micro-computer platforms. See http://en.wikipedia.org/wiki/Colossal_Cave_Adventure for more.

Columns. SEGA Master System. Developed and published by SEGA, 1990. Ported to Game Gear, Genesis, MSX, PC, SNES, and TurboGrafx-16. Numerous sequels and adaptations on many platforms.

Computer Space. Coin-op. Developed by Nolan Bushnell and Ted Dabney. Nutting Associates, 1971.

Cooking Mama. Nintendo DS. Developed by Office Create. Taito, 2006. Sequels have appeared on iPhone, Nintendo DS, and Wii.

Crazy Taxi. Dreamcast. Developed by Hitmaker. SEGA of America, 2000. Later appeared on Gamecube; a coin-op preceded the console editions in 1999, but the Dreamcast version was the most popular.

Cruel 2 B Kind. Mobile/Outdoor. Developed by Ian Bogost and Jane McGonigal, 2006. More information can be found at http://cruelgame.com.

Custer's Revenge. Atari Video Computer System (2600). Developed and published by Mystique, 1982.

Dance Dance Revolution. Coin-op, PlayStation (2001). Developed by KCE Tokyo. Konami, 1999. Multiple sequels have appeared for various home console systems, as well as for coin-op.

Debate Night. Browser. Developed and published by Powerful Robot, 2008. Available at http://www.powerfulrobot.com/games-repository/obama/.

Diner Dash. Windows, Macintosh. Developed by GameLab. PlayFirst, 2003. Multiple sequels and adaptations have appeared on various platforms.

Disaffected! Windows, Macintosh. Developed and published by Persuasive Games. Available at http://www.persuasivegames.com/games/game.aspx?game=disaffected.

Dr. Mario. Nintendo Entertainment System. Developed by Nintendo R&D1. Nintendo, 1990. Multiple sequels and adaptations have appeared on various platforms.

ESP Game. Browser. Developed and published by Games with a Purpose (GWAP). Available at http://www.gwap.com/gwap/gamesPreview/espgame/.

Eye Toy: Kinetic. PlayStation 2. Developed by SCE London Studio. Sony Computer Entertainment, 2005.

Far Cry. Windows. Developed by Crytek. Ubisoft, 2004.

FarmVille. Web/Facebook. Developed and published by Zynga, 2009. Available at http://www.facebook.com/FarmVille. Also ported to iPhone, iPad.

Final Fantasy VII. PlayStation, Windows. Developed by Square, 1997.

flOw. PlayStation 3. Developed by That Game Company. Sony Computer Entertainment, 2006.

Food Force. Windows, Macintosh. Developed by Deepend and Playerthree. United Nations World Food Programme, 2005. Available at http://www.wfp.org/how-to-help/individuals/food-force.

FrontierVille. Web/Facebook. Developed and published by Zynga, 2010. Available at http://www.facebook.com/FrontierVille.

General Retreat/Westward Ho. Atari Video Computer System (2600). Published by Playaround, circa 1983. Republished from rights purchased from the defunct Mystique.

Geometry Wars: Retro Evolved. Xbox, Xbox 360 (2005), Windows (2007). Developed by Bizarre Creations. Microsoft Game Studios, 2003. The game began as an unlockable minigame in *Project Gotham Racing 2.*

GoldWalker. iPhone. Developed by Totally Games and DigitalMill. Published by Humana Games for Health, 2010.

Grand Theft Auto III. PlayStation 2, Windows (2002), Xbox (2003). Developed by DMA Design Limited, Rockstar North, and Rockstar Vienna. Rockstar Games, 2001.

Grand Theft Auto: San Andreas. PlayStation 2, Windows (2005), Xbox (2005), Xbox 360 (2008). Developed by Rockstar North. Rockstar Games, 2004.

Gran Turismo. Play Station. Developed by Polyphony Digital Inc. Sony Computer Entertainment, 1997. Sequels have appeared for later PlayStation consoles.

Guitar Hero. PlayStation 2. Developed by Harmonix Music Systems. RedOctane, 2005. Multiple sequels have appeared on various platforms.

Guru Meditation. Atari Video Computer System (2600), iPhone. Developed and published by Ian Bogost. More information can be found at http://www.bogost.com/games/guru_meditation.shtml.

Hail to the Chimp. PlayStation 3, Xbox 360. Developed by Wideload Games. Gamecock Media Group, 2008.

Half-Life. Windows. Developed by Valve. Published by Sierra On-Line, 1998.

Half-Life 2. Macintosh, Windows, Xbox. Developed by Valve. Published by Electronic Arts, 2004.

Halo: Combat Evolved. Xbox. Developed by Bungie Studios. Microsoft Game Studios, 2001.

Hard Drivin'. Coin-op. Developed by Atari Games Applied Research Group. Atari, 1988. Later ported to various home computers and consoles.

Harvest Moon. SNES. Developed by Amccus. Pack-In-Video, 1996. Sequels have appeared on various home consoles and handheld consoles.

HumanSim. Windows. Developed and published by Virtual Heroes, Inc, 2008–. HumanSim is an ongoing platform; more information can be found at http://www.virtualheroes.com.

Hunting with Palin. Browser. Developed by Dominic A. Tocci. AddictingGames.com, 2008. http://www.addictinggames.com/huntingwithpalin.html.

Hush. Mac, Windows. Developed by Jamie Antonisse, Chris Baily, Devon Johnson, Joey Orton, and Brittany Pirello. University of Southern California, 2008.

Ice Climber. Nintendo Entertainment System. Developed and published by Nintendo, 1995.

Ico. PlayStation 2. Developed by Team Ico. Sony Computer Entertainment America, 2001.

It Takes Two. Browser. Developed by Ferry Halim. Orisinal.com, undated. Available at http://www.ferryhalim.com/orisinal/g2/two.htm.

I Wish I Were the Moon. Browser. Developed by Daniel Benmergui, 2008. Available at http://www.ludomancy.com/blog/2008/09/03/i-wish-i-were-the-moon/.

Journey to Wild Divine. Windows, Macintosh (2004). Developed and published by the Wild Divine Project, 2003. More information can be found at http://www.wilddivine.com.

Kaboom! Atari Video Computer System (2600). Developed by Larry Kaplan. Activision, 1981.

Karaoke Revolution. PlayStation 2, Xbox (2004). Developed by Harmonix Music Systems. Konami of America, 2003.

Klax. Coin-op. Developed by Dave Akers and Mark Stephen Pierce. Atari, 1989. Ported to various home computers and consoles.

Knight on the Town/Lady in Wading. Atari Video Computer System (2600). Published by Playaround, circa 1983. Republished from rights purchased from the defunct Mystique.

Kool-Aid Man. Atari Video Computer System (2600), Intellivision. Developed by M-Network. Mattel, 1983.

Leisure Suit Larry in the Land of the Lounge Lizards. Amiga, Apple II, Atari ST, DOS, Macintosh. Developed by Al Lowe and Sierra On-Line. Sierra On-Line, 1987. Sequels appeared on various home computer platforms through the 1990s.

Madden NFL '09. PlayStation 2, PlayStation 3, PSP, Xbox, Xbox 360. Developed by EA Tiburon. Electronic Arts, 2008. The *Madden NFL* series has been published since 1988 on every major platform.

Manhunt. PlayStation 2, Windows, Xbox. Developed by DMA Design Limited. Rockstar Games, 2003.

Manhunt 2. Playstation 2, PSP, Wii, Windows. Developed by Rockstar London. Rockstar Games, 2007.

Mario Battle No. 1. Nintendo Entertainment System. Developed by Myfawny Ashmore, 2000. More information can be found at http://www.year01.com/mario/.

Mark Ecko's Getting Up: Contents under Pressure. PlayStation 2, Windows, Xbox. Developed by The Collective. Atari Europe, 2006.

Mass Effect. Windows, Xbox 360. Developed by Bioware. Microsoft Game Studios, 2007.

Math Blaster! DOS. Developed and published by Davidson Associates, 1986. The series continued through 1997 on home computer and console platforms.

McDonald's Videogame. Browser. Developed and published by La Molleindustria. Available at http://www.mcvideogame.com.

Mega Man. Nintendo Entertainment System. Developed by Capcom. Capcom USA, 1987. Sequels have appeared on home console platforms through 2010.

Mega Man 9. PlayStation 3, Wii, Xbox 360. Developed by Inti Creates. Capcom Entertainment, 2008.

Metal Gear Solid. PlayStation. Developed by Konami Computer Entertainment Japan. Konami, 1998.

Microsoft Flight Simulator. PC, Macintosh (1986), DOS (1988-1994), Windows (1996-1998). Developed and published by Microsoft, 1982.

Microsoft Train Simulator. Windows. Developed by Kuju Entertainment Ltd. Microsoft, 2001.

Monopoly. Board Game. Developed by Elizabeth Magie Louis and Fred Thun (The Landlord's Game), Charles Darrow. Parker Brothers, 1935.

Monopoly Here & Now. Board Game. Developed by Parker Brothers. Hasbro, 2008. See http://en.wikipedia.org/wiki/Monopoly_Here_and_Now#World_editions for more information. Digital versions were published under license by Electronic Arts in 2010.

MVP Baseball 2003. PlayStation 2, Windows, Xbox. Developed by EA Canada. Published by Electronic Arts, 2003.

Ninja Gaiden. Nintendo Entertainment System. Developed and published by Tecmo, 1989. An Xbox update appeared in 2004.

NRA Gun Club. PlayStation 2. Developed by Jarhead Games. Creative Entertainment, 2006.

NRA Varmint Hunter. Windows. Published by Speedco Shooting Sports, 2004.

PainStation. Installation. Developed by Volker Morawe and Tilman Reiff. See http://www.painstation.de.

Palin as President. Browser. Developer unknown. http://www.palinaspresident.us.

Parallel Parking Game. Browser. Developed and published by Driver's Ed Direct, 2009. Available at http://www.driverseddirect.com/game.

Parking Wars. Browser/Facebook. Developed by Area/Code. A&E Games, 2007. Available at http://apps.facebook.com/parkingwars.

Passage. iPhone (2008), Linux, Macintosh, Windows. Developed by Jason Rohrer, 2007. Available at http://hcsoftware.sourceforge.net/passage.

Penn & Teller's Smoke and Mirrors. Sega CD. Developed by Imagineering. Absolute Entertainment, unreleased. More information can be found at http://en.wikipedia.org/wiki/Penn_%26_Teller's_Smoke_and_Mirrors.

Pet Society. Browser/Facebook. Developed and published by Playfish, 2009–.

Philly Flasher/Cathouse Blues. Atari Video Computer System (2600). Published by Playaround, circa 1983. Republished from rights purchased from the defunct Mystique.

Pikmin. GameCube. Developed by Nintendo EAD. Nintendo, 2001.

Pocketbike Racer. Xbox, Xbox 360. Developed by Blitz Arcade. King Games, 2006.

Polar Palin. Browser. Developed and published by T-Enterprise. Available at http://www.t-enterprise.co.uk/flashgame/playgame.aspx?id=polarpalin [site offline].

Pole Position. Coin-op. Developed and published by Namco, 1982. Ports appeared on many home console platforms.

Pong. Coin-op. Developed and published by Atari, 1972.

Pork Invaders. Browser. Published by John McCain for President, 2008. No longer online.

President Elect. Apple II, Commodore 64. Developed and published by Strategic Simulations, 1981.

Project Gotham Racing. Xbox. Developed by Bizarre Creations. Microsoft, 2001.

Rainmaker. Web. Developed by Ferry Halim. Orisinal.com, undated. Available at http://www.ferryhalim.com/orisinal/g2/rainmaker.htm.

RapeLay. Windows. Developed and published by Illusion, 2006.

Ravenwood Fair. Browser/Facebook. Developed and published by Lolapps, 2010. Available at http://www.facebook.com/RavenwoodFair.

Reader Rabbit. DOS, Macintosh. Developed and published by The Learning Company, 1989.

Reflect. Windows. Developed by Mike Treanor. Digital Arts and New Media MFA thesis, the University of California at Santa Cruz, 2008. Available at http://danm.ucsc.edu/~micitari/reflect.

Resistance: Fall of Man. Play Station 3, Developed by Insomniac Games, Inc., Sony Computer Entertainment America, Inc., 2006.

Rez. Dreamcast, Play Station 2, Xbox. Developed by Sega United Game Artists. Sega, 2001.

Rhythm Heaven. Nintendo DS. Developed by Nintendo. Nintendo of America, 2008.

Rock Band. PlayStation 2, PlayStation 3, Xbox 360, Wii (2008). Developed by Harmonix Music Systems. MTV Games/Electronic Arts, 2007. Several sequels have since appeared on home console platforms.

September 12th: A Toy World. Browser. Developed by Powerful Robot Games. Newsgaming.com/Powerful Robot Games, 2003. Available at http://www.newsgaming.com/games/index12.htm.

Shenmue. Dreamcast. Developed by SEGA-AM2. SEGA of America, 2000.

Silent Hill. PlayStation. Developed by Team Silent. Konami Europe, 1999.

SimCity. Amiga, Macintosh, Commodore 64. Developed by Maxis Software. Brøderbund, 1989. Later released on Atari ST (1990), BBC Micro (1990), ZX Spectrum (1990), SNES (1991), Windows 3.x (1992), Wii (2006).

SimCity 2000. DOS, Macintosh, Windows. Developed and published by Maxis Software, 1996.

SimCopter. Windows. Developed by Maxis Software. Electronic Arts, 1996.

GAMEOGRAPHY < 177 >

Singstar. PlayStation 2. Developed by SCEE Studio London. Sony Computer Entertainment Europe, 2004.

Sneak King. Xbox, Xbox 360. Developed by Blitz Arcade. King Games, 2006.

Solitaire (Microsoft Solitaire). Windows. Developed and published by Microsoft, 1990–.

Space Invaders. Coin-op. Developed by Taito. Midway, 1978.

Spacewar! PDP-1. Developed by Steve Russell, Martin Graetz, and Wayne Witaenem, 1962.

Squigl. Browser. Developed and published by Games with a Purpose (GWAP). Available at http://www.gwap.com/gwap/gamesPreview/ squigl/.

Super Mario Bros. Nintendo Entertainment System. Developed and published by Nintendo, 1985.

Super Mario Clouds. Nintendo Entertainment System. Developed by Cory Arcangel, 2002. Documented at http://www.medienkunstnetz. de/works/super-mario-cloud/

Syobon Action. Windows. Anonymous. Available at http:// www.geocities.jp/z_gundam_tanosii/home/Main.html.

Tag a Tune. Browser. Developed and published by Games with a Purpose (GWAP). Available at http://www.gwap.com/gwap/ gamesPreview/tagatune/.

Take Back Illinois. Browser. Developed by Persuasive Games. Published by the Illinois House Republican Organization, 2004. Available at http://www.takebackillinoisgame.com.

Tax Invaders. Browser. Developed and published by the Republican National Committee, 2004. No longer online.

Tennis for Two. Custom hardware. Developed by Willy Higginbotham, 1958.

Tetris. PC. Developed by Alexey Pajitnov/AcademySoft. Spectrum Holobyte, 1986. Popularized on the Nintendo Game Boy (developed by Bullet-Proof Software), published by Nintendo of America, 1989.

The Arcade Wire: Airport Security. Browser. Developed by Persuasive Games. Shockwave.com, 2006. Available at http://www.shockwave.com/gamelanding/airportsecurity.jsp.

The Getaway. PlayStation 2. Developed by SCEE Studio Soho. Sony Computer Entertainment America, 2003.

The Godfather: the Game. PlayStation 2, Windows, Xbox, Xbox 360. Developed by EA Redwood Shores, Headgate Studios. Electronic Arts, 2006.

The Grocery Game. Web. Developed by Teri Gault/The Grocery Game, Inc. Available at http://www.thegrocerygame.com.

The Landlord's Game. Board Game. Developed by Elizabeth Magie (1904). Economic Game Company of New York, 1924.

The Legend of Zelda: The Ocarina of Time. Nintendo 64. Developed by Nintendo EAD. Nintendo, 1998.

The Legend of Zelda: Twilight Princess. GameCube, Wii. Developed by Nintendo EAD. Nintendo, 2006.

The Legend of Zelda: The Wind Waker. GameCube. Developed by Nintendo EAD, 2003.

The Marriage. Windows. Developed by Rod Humble, 2007. Available at http://www.rodvik.com/rodgames/marriage.html.

The Political Machine. Windows. Developed by Stardock Systems. Ubisoft, 2004.

The Political Machine 2008. Windows. Developed and published by Stardock Systems, 2008.

The Sims. Windows, Macintosh. Developed by Maxis Software. Electronic Arts, 2000.

The Sims Online. Windows. Developed by Maxis Software. Electronic Arts, 2002.

The Storyteller. Browser. Developed by Daniel Benmergui, 2008. Available at http://www.ludomancy.com/blog/2008/09/15/ storyteller/.

Thief: The Dark Project. Windows. Developed by Looking Glass Studios. Eidos Interactive, 2008.

Tom Clancy's Splinter Cell. GameCube, Mac, PlayStation 2, Windows, Xbox. Developed by Ubisoft Montreal. Ubisoft, 2002.

Tooth Protectors. Atari Video Computer System (2600). Developed and published by DSD/Camelot, 1983.

Torture Game 2. Browser. Developed by Carl Havemann. Newgrounds. com, 2008. Available at http://www.newgrounds.com/portal/ view/439144.

True Crime: Streets of LA. GameCube, Macintosh, PlayStation 2, Windows, Xbox. Developed by LuxoFlux, EXAKT Entertainment. Activision Publishing, 2003.

Truth Invaders. Browser. Developed by Jeremy Bernstein, Vince Diamante, Duane Dunfield, Sean Nadeau, Angi Shearstone, 2008. Available at http://www.truthinvaders.com.

Viva Piñata. Xbox 360. Developed by Rare. Microsoft Game Studios, 2006.

Wario Ware: Smooth Moves. Wii. Developed by Intelligent Systems. Nintendo of America, 2007.

WarioWare, Inc.: Mega Microgame$! Game Boy Advance. Developed by Nintendo R&D1. Nintendo, 2003.

Where Is My Heart. Windows, Macintosh. Developed by Bernhard Schulenburg, 2008. Available at http://bushghost.blogspot.com.

White House Joust. Browser. Developed and published by KewlBox. com, 2004. Available online at http://kewlbox.com/games/ gameDetail.aspx?gameID=282 [2008 edition].

Wii Fit. Wii. Developed by Nintendo EAD. Nintendo of America, 2008.

Wii Sports. Wii. Developed and published by Nintendo, 2006.

World of Warcraft. Windows, Macintosh. Developed and published by Blizzard Entertainment, 2004–.

World without Oil. Alternate Reality Game. Developed by Ken Eklund et al. Independent Television Service, 2007. Archive available at http://www.worldwithoutoil.org.

Zidane Head-Butt. Browser. AddictingGames.com, 2006. Available at http://www.addictinggames.com/zidaneheadbuttgame.html.

Zork: The Great Underground Empire. Amiga, Amstrad CPC, Apple II, Atari 8-bit, Atari ST, Commodore 64. Developed by Marc Blank, Dave Lebling, Bruce Daniels and Tim Anderson. Infocom, 1980. Released for many more platforms in the 1980s, and via Z-Machine readers thereafter.

Zuma Deluxe. Macintosh, Mobile (various), Windows. Developed and published by PopCap Games, 2003. Later released on PlayStation 3, Xbox, Xbox 360.

IAN BOGOST is an award-winning videogame designer and media philosopher. He is professor of digital media at the Georgia Institute of Technology, as well as founding partner at Persuasive Games LLC. He is author or coauthor of several books, including *Unit Operations: An Approach to Videogame Criticism, Persuasive Games: The Expressive Power of Videogames, Racing the Beam: The Atari Video Computer System,* and *Newsgames: Journalism at Play.* His videogames have been exhibited internationally and played by millions of people; they cover topics as varied as airport security, disaffected workers, the petroleum industry, suburban errands, and tort reform. His most recent game, *A Slow Year,* a collection of game poems for Atari, won the Vanguard and Virtuoso awards at the 2010 Indiecade Festival. For more information, go to www.bogost.com.

Electronic Mediations

Katherine Hayles, Mark Poster, and Samuel Weber, Series Editors